EFFECTIVE
BIBLE STUDY

EFFECTIVE
BIBLE STUDY

by
HOWARD F. VOS

ZONDERVAN
PUBLISHING HOUSE
OF THE ZONDERVAN CORPORATION
GRAND RAPIDS, MICHIGAN 49506

EFFECTIVE BIBLE STUDY
Copyright 1956 by
Zondervan Publishing House
Grand Rapids, Michigan

Eighteenth printing   1978
ISBN 0-310-33851-4

Printed in the United States of America

To My Parents

PREFACE

While the writer was teaching in Chattanooga, one of his former students sent him an urgent plea for information concerning methods of Bible study. Thus was rekindled a dormant interest, and the result was two Bible study methods courses offered at Tennessee Temple College.

During the three years I was teaching these courses, my students enrolled evidenced such a growth in spiritual insight and knowledge of the Word that I became increasingly impressed with the value of passing on some of these procedures to others.

The author's aim in writing this book, then, is to set forth principles of Bible study which have been developed and proved by students and teacher, with the hope that they will be useful to other students and laymen in their efforts to attain a better grasp of the truth of God as revealed in His Word.

HOWARD F. VOS

Evanston, Illinois

ACKNOWLEDGMENTS

The author wishes to thank the following publishers for permission to use copyrighted material:

Moody Press, for quotations from *How to Prepare Sermons and Gospel Addresses* by William Evans.

Scott, Foresman & Co., for quotations from *Principles and Types of Speech* by Alan H. Monroe.

University of Chicago Press, for quotations from *The Complete Bible,* translated by Smith and Goodspeed.

W. A. Wilde Company, for quotations from *Profitable Bible Study* by Wilbur M. Smith.

William B. Eerdmans Publishing Co., for quotations from *Galatians: The Charter of Christian Liberty* by Merrill C. Tenney.

CONTENTS

CHAPTER I

INTRODUCTION

John the Baptist was a voice crying in the wilderness. Few Christians today are anything but an echo. Repetition of profound Biblical truths discovered by a Spurgeon or a Moody or a Morgan has become the accepted practice. Many wish for the ability to utter beautiful thoughts like these great men of years gone by but fail to discern God's richest blessings because they are not willing to pay the price for discovering them. Others may have the ambition and perseverance but lack the knowledge of how to go about finding gems in the Word for themselves.

(The deeper things of the Word are not reserved for a few special individuals but are available to all who will search for them. The fact that all may plumb the depths of Spiritual truth does not mean that they may do so without effort, however. Seeking a shortcut is a great curse of the hour; there are no shortcuts to a real knowledge of the Word.) The "Spanish in Twenty Easy Lessons" philosophy does not work with God. (Hard work and a dependence upon the teaching ministry of the Holy Spirit are the only avenues through which success in this field is achieved. But diligence and the teaching ministry of the Holy Spirit may not advance one too far if he has no definite plan. One may spend many hours in toil and discover that he has been going in circles; the teaching ministry of the Holy Spirit may be operative but only to the extent of providing scattered items that need to be tied together by an integrated plan.)

Probably one of the greatest faults of the strictly conservative constituency of the United States is that it puts much emphasis on doing things for God and getting into the Word of God but not much emphasis on the "how" of accomplishment. If the "how-to-do-it" articles in magazines and the "how-to-do-it" kits on the shelves of stores are having such great success, why shouldn't much stress be put on the "how" with regard to Bible study? Certainly there is a very real need for literature on how to study the Bible — literature that will serve the layman in his search for greater Biblical knowledge, the preacher who wishes to have a truly Bible-centered ministry, and the teacher in a Bible institute, Bible college, or Christian liberal arts college who is looking for a textbook in this field. It is to this end that the present work is written — not as the last word on the subject but as a brief introduction.[1]

Plenty of books are available on Greek and Hebrew exegesis and a general understanding of the original languages. The present one seeks to provide a guide for a student of the English Bible. The general plan of each of the chapters of this book is as follows: first the method is defined. In the case of such methods as the theological, sociological, political and philosophical, an effort is made to provide an outline or a brief survey of those fields of knowledge so that the reader will be able to keep at a minimum his research into non-Biblical materials and will in that measure be free to concentrate more on the message of Scripture.

Second, an example is developed. In this way the student can see in action the principles which were set forth in the definition. Third, where it seems that it would be helpful to include them, suggestions are made for further study. These are listed so that the layman may continue study on his own and the teacher who may use this book for a text will have assignment topics from which to choose.[2] Lastly, a helpful bibliog-

---

[1] The writer recognizes that there have been helpful works written on the subject of methods of Bible study. One of the best is *Galatians: The Charter of Christian Liberty*, by Dr. Merrill C. Tenney, Dean of the Graduate School, Wheaton College, Wheaton, Ill. Dr. Tenney uses nine methods in his study of the book of Galatians.

[2] Note Appendix I for suggested classroom procedure which the teacher might utilize when teaching a course for which this book has been selected as a text.

raphy is provided either in footnotes or at the end of many of the chapters. In many cases, however, these bibliographical aids are not necessary to a study of the method. It is hoped that in most cases these methods will enable the believer to go directly to the Word without helps.)

In an effort to provide a few useful pointers on proclaiming some of the truths discovered by means of these methods, (a concluding chapter is added on the subject of methods of teaching the Bible.)No attempt is made to be original at this point because so much has been written on the subject, but a great deal of that which has been written is out of print or in some other way made inaccessible to the average Christian.

A warning must be sounded here. (Let no one think that he can take a set of rules or suggestions for study of the Bible and arrive at divine truth. Study plans are no substitution for the teaching ministry of the Holy Spirit, which is promised in John 16:13-15, "Howbeit when he, the Spirit of truth, is come, he will guide you into all truth: for he shall not speak of himself; but whatsoever he shall hear, that shall he speak: and he will shew you things to come. He shall glorify me: for he shall receive of mine, and shall shew it unto you. All things that the Father hath are mine: therefore said I, that he shall take of mine, and shall shew it unto you.")

Further(let it be observed that this teaching ministry is not available to everyone. The unsaved man cannot expect to know it because "the natural man receiveth not the things of the Spirit of God: for they are foolishness unto him: neither can he know them, because they are spiritually discerned" (I Cor. 2:14, AV). Again, the carnal or unspiritual Christian will not come into the fullness of God's truth because he is a babe in Christ who must be fed with milk and not with the meat of the Word (I Cor. 3:1, 2). Rather, it is only the spiritual man — the one in right relationship to the Lord — who can claim the teaching power of the Spirit. Paul states by inspiration, "But as it is written, Eye hath not seen, nor ear heard, neither have entered into the heart of man, the things which God hath prepared for them that love him. But God hath revealed them unto us

by his Spirit: for the Spirit searcheth all things, yea, the deep
things of God" (I Cor. 2:9, 10, AV).

To the one who may be classified as a spiritual Christian,
there are plenty of admonitions to the effect that disobedience
to the light will result in a taking away of the light and re-
placing it with darkness. Mark 4:23-25 is a case in point.
There Jesus in talking to His disciples remarks, "If any man
have ears to hear, let him hear . . . Take heed what ye
hear: with what measure ye mete, it shall be measured to you:
and unto you that hear shall more be given. For he that hath,
to him shall be given: and he that hath not, from him shall
be taken even that which he hath" (AV). This passage emphasizes the truth of total obedience on the part of the believer — whether the obedience be expressed by the hands,
the feet, the heart, or the lips. In proportion to our submis-
sion the Lord will give greater blessing, opportunity, and light;
unfaithfulness on the other hand will result in deprivation of
the light. This truth is also brought to our attention in John
15:14-15: "Ye are my friends, if ye do whatsoever I command
you. Henceforth I call you not servants; for the servant
knoweth not what his lord doeth: but I have called you
friends; for all things that I have heard of my Father I have
made known unto you." The Lord here expresses the thought
that the one who complies with His commands will have the
relationship to Him that close friends sustain here on earth —
they enter intimately into each other's plans, problems, and
hopes. Whenever a matter comes between them, however,
the fellowship is broken; and they no longer enjoy that com-
monality of interests. In other words, when we fail to follow
the commands of Christ, our fellowship with Him is broken
and He no longer tells us all things He has heard of the
Father. In this regard, G. Campbell Morgan aptly remarks,
"The Divine Library is a revelation, and a revelation means
light, and light means an unveiling of the things of darkness,
accompanied by a demand that they should be put away.
. . . but if we persist in the things against which we are
warned, the Bible becomes a sealed book, and we can neither

know it, nor teach it."[3] The same thought is expressed in the couplet:

> Light obeyed increaseth light,
> Light rejected bringeth night.)

(Not only must the believer be careful to respond to the light, but he should also recognize that the study of the Bible requires honesty. That is, prejudice cannot be allowed to play any part in a perusal of the Word; one has no right to twist the truth to fit his own preconceived opinions. Approach the Bible with an open mind; make it your own — let it not be the Bible of parents, teachers, or preachers who have prejudiced you concerning certain facets of truth. Allow the Bible to speak for itself.

May it be the portion of all who read this book that they find themselves in constant and blessed fellowship with the risen and glorified Lord so that the Comforter whom He promised to send will be able to shed divine light on the sacred page and lead the believer into the unsearchable riches of the Word.

[3] G. Campbell Morgan, *The Study and Teaching of the English Bible,* (London: James Clarke & Co.), pp. 79, 80.

Chapter II

THE INDUCTIVE METHOD

It is the privilege of every believer to go directly to the Word and find therein the clear-cut message of truth. The practice of running to a commentary before studying the Bible itself gives a definite direction to one's study and a cast to his thinking which may lead him to conclusions never intended by the Holy Spirit. Further, the individual deprives himself of the blessing of discovering eternal verities for himself. After all, those who wrote the commentaries had to get their material in the same way any present-day Bible student can get it. It should not be necessary for the Christian constantly to depend on the Biblical research of another; he should seek a spiritual maturity that will enable him to get beyond this stage. The inductive method is in a peculiar way designed to enable one to develop rapidly in the ability to do independent Bible study.

THE METHOD DEFINED

It must be recognized at the outset that the methods detailed in this book may be somewhat arbitrarily named and that others will assign terms more to their liking. Moreover, it is difficult to prevent overlapping in these studies; in developing one method there will be frequent utilization of aspects of others. The name which the writer chooses for the present study is the inductive method because emphasis is placed on the process of reasoning or drawing conclusions from particular cases. Involved are inquiry, investigation, scrutiny, and a great deal of stress on observation.

Others may prefer to entitle this approach the "book method" because the method is best utilized when applied to a whole book. But it must be said that induction can be used on any

16

portion of a book and that a book method might primarily employ the analytical, synthetic, or other types of study. Again, the title "paragraph method" could be assigned because particular emphasis is laid on the paragraph as the unit of study. Or, one might choose to call it the "compositive method" since much stress is put upon the literary composition or verbal expression of the text.

Whatever the name, the system is the same. And remember that system is the essence of Bible study; no one is in any sense a Bible student who takes up the Bible and reads it in a haphazard way, looking at a page here and there. The orderly development of this method requires that first of all the book to be studied be read through at one sitting and without interruption. Only in this way is it possible to discover the main outlines of a book. Since the writer had a primary message to impart to the reader, and since the Bible is good literature, a quality of which is the orderly development of thought progression, it may be taken for granted that a modern reader can locate the places where the argument of the writer takes a slightly different turn or where he begins a new angle of the development of his theme. It is preferable to read a book through several times before beginning any more serious study of it. After reading the book carefully, jot down the main divisions as you believe them to be. Next, by means of continued rereading assign sub-points to these main points of the outline. All of this reading should be done in a Bible, such as the American Standard Version, that divides the text into paragraphs, as the paragraph will be the main unit of study. It is imperative also that the Bible be without editorial comment so the reader will be free to form his own conclusions on the basis of what he finds.

The outline having been established, it is now possible to begin detailed study of the book. Let the verses which appear after the first sub-point in the outline constitute the initial unit of study. Observe! Do not merely look but scrutinize, analyze, and digest the text. Stay with the portion until your *looking* becomes *seeing*. It would be a good exercise to spend one hour digging in the first paragraph. What do you see that you never noticed there before? Record the answers to this question. Be inquisitive; learn to ask yourself questions. Put the six honest serving men to work for you: Who? What? When? Where? Why? and How?

In succeeding paragraphs of the section and book constantly try to determine why the paragraph is in the book, and why it is where it is. Study the people to see if you can learn why they are mentioned, their connection with the main character or characters, and the similarities or contrasts between the principals of the story. Geographical locations and time elements are included for a reason; what do they contribute to the narrative or the doctrine set forth here? A sanctified imagination is a help to anyone. What do you feel, see, hear, or smell? Then try looking at the text from the standpoint of an artist, dramatist, musician, sportsman, housewife, or an individual in some other walk of life; live the passage as one with such an occupation would live it.

It is important to compare Scripture with Scripture. That is a primary rule of Scriptural interpretation. One can make gross errors by failing to see a teaching in the light of its immediate context or what the Bible as a whole has to say about it.

Next ask the question, What does this paragraph, section or book teach? And in answering this question, as well as the rest here suggested for study, keep interpretation, application and devotionalizing at a minimum; stick with what the text *says*.

One more important development of this method remains. That is the matter of charting. Charting enables one to organize and visualize the essential material which he finds in a book or any part of it. The simplest way to chart is to place across the top of the sheet the main divisions; on the next line place the section headings (sub-points in the outline); then place the paragraph names on slanting lines between the section headings and the main body of the chart. Now along the left margin of the page list the subjects you wish to trace through the book, such as God, Christ, prayer, etc. When lines are drawn down from the top of the page in places where divisions come between the section headings and horizontally between the subjects traced, convenient boxes will be available for notations concerning the development of the subject in that particular section. It is hoped that the following illustration will present a clear picture of this.

DIVISIONS					
SECTIONS					
Paragraphs					
SUBJECTS TO BE					
TRACED					

EXAMPLE OF METHOD

The impossibility of presenting a detailed example of this method should readily be recognized, for the inductive method calls for a consideration of every item of Scripture. It would take an entire volume, then, to demonstrate what could be done with a single book of the Bible. Mark is selected for the present study because it has a simple, narrative style and is arranged in chronological order.[1] For the first assignment the student should be asked to read through the book at one sitting in order to discover the general outline, to find some of the main characteristics of the book, and to spend at least a half hour looking at Mark 1:1. Probably one of two conclusions will be reached by the class relative to the over-all outline: either they will decide that the book falls into three parts — 1:1-13; 1:14-8:30; 8:31-16:20 — or into several parts based on the geographical development of the book, such as ministry in Galilee, Judea, and Jerusalem, etc. The points in the threefold division could

[1] Teachers will find it possible to finish the study of Mark in a one term course of two semester hours or three quarter hours. It is difficult to cover more than about a half chapter during a class period.

be labeled the Preparation, Proclamation, and Passion. Then, as further study is carried out in the book, the sectional divisions will become apparent. By way of example, names for those appearing in the first few chapters could be assigned as follows: Introduction of Jesus, 1:1-8; Preparation of Jesus, 1:9-13; Launching of Ministry, 1:14-45; Beginning of Opposition, 2:1-3:6; Organizing of Forces 3:7-35; and A Day of Kingdom Parables, 4:1-41.

Once the sectional divisions are determined, the instructor can make assignments by sections or the Bible student can work out his study program in the same manner. A threefold plan should be developed for the student: 1. Naming the paragraphs appearing in the unit assigned;[2] 2. Making ten original observations on the text; 3. Answering questions composed by the instructor.[3] If this method is utilized for class study, it is suggested that occasionally the students be allowed to make their own questions based on observations on the portion under consideration.

This method has been called the inductive — drawing conclusions or generalizations from particular, learning to tabulate observations relating to the same general subject and drawing conclusions therefrom. A few examples should clarify this point. In Mark 1:1 various names for the Lord are given. It may be "looking" to note that the names exist, but "seeing" demands detailed consideration of them. "Jesus" is the human name; "Christ" means *anointed*, and therefore denotes the fact that He was on a mission; "Son of God" proclaims that He was divine. Taken together, these names give a full account of the person of Christ — a divine-human being on a mission. Verses two and three go on to tell that He came in fulfillment of prophecy.

A further observation may be made relative to Peter in 1: 14-45. Verse sixteen speaks of Andrew as being his brother; verses thirty and thirty-one describe the healing of Simon's mother-in-law; and in verse thirty-six there was already an in-

---

[2] In naming paragraphs, one should strive to compose a title consisting of three words or less, one which will be descriptive of the content of the paragraph, and one which will differentiate this paragraph from all the other paragraphs of the book.

[3] A sample list of questions is provided later in this chapter.

timation that Simon led the group. The conclusion drawn is that he is already in a position of leadership among the disciples, and the reader may expect to see him in action often later in the book. Endless observations can be made concerning truths latent in the Gospel of Mark, but other aspects of the method are yet to be mentioned.

Study by means of comparison often brings out much spiritual truth. Note the two feasts of chapter six: one held by Herod when John the Baptist was beheaded and the other by Jesus when He fed the five thousand. Compare the two under the headings of Host, Occasion, Provision, Guests, Type of Entertainment, Location, Attitude of Those Gathered, and Result. It would also be interesting to compare the feeding of the five thousand and the four thousand according to number present, location of crowd, time element, food available at the beginning of the meal, and fragments left over. Still another good comparison is provided in the persons of John the Baptist and Jesus. Note their parentage, purpose of their ministry, nature of their ministry, attitude of people toward them, their appearance, and the way in which they suffered death.

Mention was made earlier in this chapter that the instructor should compose a list of questions to accompany each assignment made in a book which the class might be studying. Perhaps it would be well to include here a sample list of questions to give some idea of what kind of thing can be done with them. This list relates to Mark 1:14-45.

1. Study the section carefully, making observations and giving titles to paragraphs.
2. Notice the relation of paragraphs to each other. Why put the paragraph in? Why put it where it is?
3. Study notations of time and place. What do they contribute to the development of the section?
4. Be prepared to discuss from this section the problems confronting Jesus.
5. What reactions toward Him are recorded?
6. What changes were brought about by Him?
7. What centers of life did He touch?

The instructor should always remember that the secret of the success of this method is not to dish out facts to a group of students but to lead them by good study questions and class questions to discover for themselves what the Word contains.

During his study of a book in private or in school, the student has been taking copious notes and amassing tremendous numbers of facts, but these are of relatively little value unless they are organized into some sensible relationship. This is accomplished by means of the chart. Charting is valuable because it makes possible a view of the whole book at a glance, enabling one to get at the contents and main thoughts; it states whole concepts concisely — in a word or two; and it acts as a memory clue. The mechanics of the chart have already been mentioned, but something must be said here about subjects that may be traced through the book. Study Jesus' identity. What names are attributed to Him in the book? What does He claim to be and do? Then note His opposition. What does the book say about the Twelve? What miracles are listed? What parables does Jesus deliver? List the teachings relative to the kingdom of God. For example, in chapter one Jesus is the bringer of the kingdom; in chapter four, He teaches concerning the kingdom; chapter nine presents a glimpse into the future kingdom; chapter ten teaches that entrance into the kingdom will be by means of the humility of a child; in chapter eleven the King enters Jerusalem; chapter 13 speaks of the second coming of the King; and in chapter fifteen Joseph appears as the seeker of the kingdom. Teachings on the Holy Spirit, prayer, Mark's use of the Old Testament, and the attitude toward women in the book also are interesting subjects to trace through this Gospel.

SUGGESTIONS FOR FURTHER STUDY

Of course this method will work for any book of the Bible, but some books will produce greater results than others. Longer books, such as Genesis, would require prodigious charts; books like Proverbs, Psalms, and some historical books, change subject a little too often; Zechariah, Daniel, Ezekiel, and some of the other prophetic books have language which is highly figurative in spots and which presents a basic problem in interpretation. Others, as Nehemiah and Jonah, may be studied better from the biographical standpoint. Ruth and Esther make good narrative expositions. The method works best when the book is of moderate length and does not present too many thorny problems of interpretation.

First Samuel, Romans, and Hebrews are three of the books which adapt themselves well to the inductive method. A careful reading of I Samuel will probably demonstrate that the main divisions are the early life and ministry of Samuel, the anointing and early years of Saul, the anointing of David and his struggles with Saul. Some of the interesting subjects which may be traced through the book and charted are prayer, the Holy Spirit, the results of sin, what is revealed of God, and what may be learned of the nation of Israel. Special subjects of study which will well repay the student's effort are a contrast of Eli and Samuel, and Saul and David, a comparison of Samuel and David, tracing of the steps in the downfall of Saul, and an investigation into the qualities of character in the person of David.

Though an unfathomable book, Romans also makes an excellent subject for an inductive study. The reader will discover that the main divisions of the text will differ according to the ideas emphasized in the initial survey of the book. One simple outline consists of two points: Doctrinal, chapters 1-11; Practical, chapters 12-16. Since this is the greatest doctrinal book of the Bible, most of the items to be traced on the chart will be doctrinal in nature. Note especially justification, condemnation, righteousness, the sovereignty of God, the Holy Spirit, death in its various ramifications, the flesh, the Law, and God's relationship to the Jew and to the lost. Of course, the student is expected to trace these subjects through the book by means of his personal contact with the book, but the use of a concordance will prove to be very helpful. Some further topics for development are the believer's two natures (chapter 7), the comparison or relationship of the Jew, Gentile, and the Church, and the saint's responsibilities (chapters

12-15). The latter may be studied under the headings of Religious Duties (chapter 12), Civil Duties (chapter 13), and Fraternal Duties in Matters of Conscience (chapters 14 and 15).

A third book of the Bible upon which an inductive study may be performed is Hebrews. Like Romans, it may well be divided into a doctrinal and a practical section: The Glory of the Person and Work of Christ, 1:1 - 10:18; The Application, 10:19 - 13:25. According to the judgment of the reader, other outlines may be formulated. For example, consider the following by Martin O. Massinger, president of the Dallas Bible Institute, Dallas, Texas.

1. God's final revelation of Himself in Christ, 1:1-3
2. Christ's superiority over angels, 1:4 - 2:18
3. Christ's superiority over Moses, 3:1 - 4:13
4. Christ's superiority over Aaron and the Levitical priesthood, 4:14 - 10:18
5. Exhortations based on the fact of Christ's superiority over all else, 10:19 - 13:25

A few topics which may be traced through the book with great blessing are the "better" things, the many occurrences of the exhortation "Let us," or "Let"; the words "perfect," "heavenly," "eternal"; the subject of typology (some of the greatest types are the priesthood, the sacrificial lamb, and the tabernacle); and salvation. Now make out a list of other subjects which will repay some honest toil. No doubt you have somewhere near the top the problem passages relating to the subject of the eternal security of the believer, the doctrine of faith, and the teachings in the book concerning angels.

Chapter III

THE SYNTHETIC METHOD

William Evans aptly observes, "The Bible was made bookwise — one book at a time, according as the need for the truth, historical, prophetical or ethical, as set forth therein, arose."[1] Of course, a high view of inspiration does not demand that an author of Scripture sit down and pen an entire book at a sitting or within a few days, but it is true that each book constitutes a unit embodying a primary message which can be discovered only when the book is studied as a whole. The present-day division of books into verses, paragraphs, and chapters was not characteristic of the original manuscripts; though there were undoubtedly divisions or stops of thought marked by transitions or by definite statements of change of topic in the earliest manuscripts.

Current sectionalization of Scripture is employed for the sake of convenience only, and it is not intended that the divisions should obscure the over-all message. The book is still a unit and must be studied in that manner. Synthesis, then, as the name implies, is the "putting together of a book" or the consideration of it as a whole. This is the direct opposite of analysis, which attempts to partition a book into small units of study for the purpose of detailed investigation.

There also is a distinction to be made between the inductive and synthetic view of Scripture. In the former, conclusions are drawn on the basis of detailed observation; in the latter general impressions are gained by means of less detailed investigation, and the ramifications of those main ideas are not followed out in detail. A greater explanation of the difference will be demonstrated as this present chapter progresses.

[1] William Evans, *The Book Method of Bible Study*, (Chicago: Moody Press, 1915), p. 7.

The synthetic method of Bible study relates to the whole field of Biblical investigation as a general survey does to the more specialized studies of various areas of secular knowledge. In a large proportion of American colleges and universities the student first takes History of Civilization and then branches out into a consideration of American, European, South American, or some other course in history. The geographer starts with the globe and then proceeds to learn about continents, nations, rivers, and mountains. The archeologist first makes a general survey of a mound and then stakes it out into sections and finally comes to a careful analysis of the contents of one section at a time. It is not unusual to find individuals who attack their study in reverse by learning first the rivers, mountains, plains, and the location of cities and towns and finally integrating this mass of material by relating it to countries and ultimately to continents and hemispheres. All too common is the Bible reader who flips open his Bible to a chapter or verse here and there without seeing any relationship that it may have to a book, Testament, or the whole gamut of revelation.

Perhaps some general suggestions for the development of this method are in order at this point.

1. Read the book through several times, and let each reading be at one sitting. It is not necessary that these readings follow one another in close proximity.

2. In each reading emphasize a different aspect of study, such as the geographical, historical, or doctrinal.

3. Recognize the fact that just as the book was revealed and inspired through the instrumentality of the Holy Spirit, it will likewise be illuminated by the Holy Spirit. Therefore, read prayerfully and reverently.

4. Read without helps.

5. As you read *look, listen* and *live*. Look carefully at what you are reading; listen to what the words say; and live in the time and atmosphere created by the reading of the book.

Encouragement has been offered here to read the book through often, but no definitive plan for how to do this reading has been set forth. In dealing with the synthetic method, Merrill C. Tenney in his study of Galatians recommends that in the first reading one should look for the central theme and note how the author seeks to develop it; one should look for a key verse or passage which generally embodies the central theme. In the second reading, the reader should keep the central theme in mind and try to see the ways in which this theme is emphasized throughout the book. The tone of the book should also be defined: is it didactic, polemic, or what is it? In the same reading, special problems or interests dealt with in the book should be noted. In the third or fourth reading, the reader should develop the outline.[2] This threefold plan is adopted in the present chapter.

Certainly intelligence is an attribute of deity, and God the Holy Spirit inspired the Bible; in the process of inspiration the human element is not omitted — and man is a rational being. It may be concluded, then, that since intelligent beings produced Scripture each book must have a logical plan, as do other pieces of literature. If each book has a primary message arranged according to rhetorical principles, it should be possible for the general reader to discover the plan. Sometimes there is an announcement of a change of subject as in I Corinthians with the repetition of "as touching" or "now concerning" in 7:1; 7:25; 8:1, 4; 12:1; 16:1; 16:12. Again, a change of subject may be obvious but unannounced. Occasionally the repetition of certain like or similar words provides a clue. Sometimes chronological, geographical, or historical divisions may be made. For instance, many like to outline certain of the Gospels according to the geographical development of Jesus' ministry — such as the Perean, Judean, Galilean ministries and the last week around Jerusalem. A most helpful way of discovering these shifts of emphasis or change of subject is to study the text by paragraphs, as set up in the American Standard Version or some other version.

DEVELOPMENT OF EXAMPLE

The first reading — the main theme. The study of the Book of Philippians has been selected as an example of this method.

[2] Merrill C. Tenney, *Galatians: The Charter of Christian Liberty* (Grand Rapids: Wm. B. Eerdmans Publishing Co., 1950), pp. 26-31.

To many who read this epistle, "joy" or "rejoicing" will seem to be the central theme. They may come to this conclusion because lurking in the back of their minds is the oft-repeated assertion that this is the message of the book; or they might decide that such is the case on the basis of the several references in the book which deal with that general subject.[3] It is the writer's belief, however, that the object of this book is twofold: the first is to thank the Philippian believers for their generous gift; but the second and more important seems to be to deal with dissension which had arisen there and which threatened the peace of the church in the community. Apparently Epaphroditus had brought Paul word of this when he presented the gift to Paul. The Apostle does not come out and deal bluntly with the whole matter of unity, but the reader will find constant allusions to the problem throughout the book. Several verses include the phrase "you all" or the word "all" and indicate that the Apostle is emphasizing the fact that he is speaking to the whole Philippian church and not several factions.[4] Consider also other references to his desire for unity, as expressed in the words "one" or "same"[5] and his command in 2:14, "Do all things without murmurings and disputings." A passage which, probably more than any other, expresses the thought of the entire epistle and therefore serves as the key is 2:1-5.[6] There one finds the basis for unity — blessings of the Christian life; the exhortation to unity — "be of the same mind"; and the means of unity — humility and the consideration of the needs of others.

Second reading — further development of the theme. Now read the book through the second time with the central thought

[3] 1:4, 18, 25, 26; 2:2, 16, 18; 3:1, 3; 4:1, 4, 10.
[4] 1:1, 4, 7, 8, 25; 2:17, 26.
[5] 1:27; 2:2; 3:16; 4:2.
[6] Perhaps the reader would enjoy the fine translation of Philippians 2:1-5 which Smith and Goodspeed provide in their *Complete Bible* (University of Chicago Press, 1939). "So by whatever appeal there is in our relation to Christ, by whatever incentive there is in love, by whatever participation there is in the Spirit, whatever affection and sympathy, make me perfectly happy by living in harmony, with the same attitude of love, with the same feeling and purpose. Do not act for selfish ends or from vanity, but modestly treat one another as your superiors. Do not take account of your own interests, but of the interests of others as well. Have the same attitude that Christ Jesus had."

in mind in order to see how the theme of unity is developed throughout the book. Paul begins the epistle with a salutation "to all the saints in Christ Jesus that are in Philippi." This is a different approach from that employed in his other letters to churches, with the exception of Romans, where he also emphasizes "all." The reason for doing so in Romans, however, seems to be that the Apostle desires to give a unity to the Roman Christian community which consists of churches meeting in a number of private homes. The author then continues to emphasize the theme in making prayer for "you all" (Phil. 1:4); in believing that the Lord would keep "you all" unto the day of Christ (1:7); in declaring his concern for "you all" (1:8); in stating that it is needful for him to abide with "you all" (1:25); in exhorting them to stand fast in one spirit, striving for the faith of the Gospel (1:27), and to live with singleness of purpose and love and without faction (2:2); his rejoicing is with "you all" (2:17); Epaphroditus shared Paul's concern for "you all" (2:26); a further emphasis on single-mindedness is found in 3:15, 16; and in 4:2 he exhorts two women who seem to be ringleaders in factional strife to put away their differences.

Of course, the greatest passage in the whole book is 2:1-11. While it is a great Christological declaration, it must be seen here in connection with the fact that all division will cease and harmony will be restored when men will have the mind of Christ and live with such a humility of life that they will not infringe upon the rights of others. When such encroachment ceases on the part of all, unity will be restored.

The tone of the book may be described as paternal. He does not particularly scold them, so the term *polemic* would not be *á propos;* nor does the Apostle enter into detailed teaching, so *didactic* would not exactly fit. He does, however, treat them as his children in the Lord and thanks them for their care of him and encourages them to quit their fussing and learn to get along better. Note the fatherly care demonstrated in 1:8, "For God is my witness, how I long after you all in the tender mercies of Christ Jesus." Then the Apostle speaks of their obedience to him in 2:12a, "So then, my beloved, even as ye have always obeyed, not as in my presence only, but now much more in my absence." Again, in 3:17 he asks them to imitate him — as would a son following in his father's steps.

In conjunction with the general theme of unity, two special problems arise. The first of these relates to Judaism and Judaizers; this is dealt with in 3:1-7. The second of the issues that had caused at least a part of the disunity was the matter of Christian perfection; that is emphasized in several passages. In answer, Paul clearly teaches that it is not absolute but progressive. Chapter three provides the most extended treatment of the subject (vv. 7-15). Observe especially some key verses of this section: "Not that I have already obtained, or am already made perfect: but I press on. . . . Brethren, I count not myself yet to have laid hold . . . I press on toward the goal. . . . Let us therefore, as many as are perfect [mature Christians], be thus minded . . ." (vv. 12-15). Other verses reflect the same teaching: ". . . he who *began* a good work in you *will perfect* it until the day of Jesus Christ" (1:6). "And this I pray, that your love may abound yet more and more in knowledge and all discernment" (1:9) indicates that they have not as yet arrived; while "that ye may become blameless and harmless . . ." (2:15) gives the same thought.

The third reading — the outline. In the third reading the outline is developed. The surest way of discovering the outline of a book is probably by means of paragraph study. The American Standard Version is helpful here. While the paragraphing of the original languages of the Bible is not inspired, it does conveniently divide the text into blocks of thought which aid the student in his search for evidences of change of subject and turns of thought that are helpful in establishing an outline. For the most part, the ASV follows the paragraphing of the original languages. Now take a sheet of paper and divide it into three vertical columns; in the first put the paragraph number; in the second list the verses covered by the paragraph; and in the third write a word or brief phrase to describe the content of that paragraph. Philippians developed in this way might look as follows.

A CHART OF PARAGRAPHS IN PHILIPPIANS
(according to the American Standard Version)

Paragraph Number	Biblical Reference	Content
1	1:1, 2	Salutation
2	1:3-11	Paul's Prayer
3	1:12-30	Paul's Imprisonment for Furtherance of Gospel
4	2:1-11	Mind of Christ
5	2:12-18	Running in Vain
6	2:19-30	Timothy's qualities; Epaphroditus' Illness, Concern
7	3:1-16	Loss for Christ
8	3:17-21	Imitators of Paul
9	4:1	Standing fast
10	4:2, 3	Help those Women
11	4:4-7	Prayer and Resultant Peace
12	4:8, 9	Controlled Thought Life
13	4:10-20	Thanksgiving and Christian Giving
14	4:21, 22	Greeting
15	4:23	Benediction

It remains now to construct an outline on the basis of the paragraph development and in line with the theme discovered in the first reading.[7] It will be noticed in the following outline that for the most part each point in the outline covers one paragraph of the text.

PHILIPPIANS: AN APPEAL FOR CHRISTIAN UNITY
Introduction: 1:1-11[8]

A. Salutation to *all*, 1:1, 2
B. Prayer for *all*, 1:3-11

I. Paul's Imprisonment As Related to the Question of Unity, 1:12-30

---

[7] Suggestions for outlining are made in Appendix II at the end of this book.
[8] A detailed outline study of Philippians is provided in *His in Joyous Experience* by Norman B. Harrison.

A. Permission of disunity in motives for evangelistic work, 1:12-20
B. Preservation to enable a continuation of growth in grace, 1:21-26
C. Exhortation to unity while he yet remains in prison for a time, 1:27-30

II. The Mind of Christ: The Source of All Unity, 2:1-30
   A. Nature: Humility of spirit, 2:1-11
     1. Obedient even unto death
     2. Exaltation by the Father
   B. Product: Unity and its results, 2:12-18
   C. Examples: Those who possess the mind of Christ, 2: 19-30
     1. Timothy
     2. Epaphroditus

III. The Biographical Appeal for Unity: Answers from Paul's Experience to the Problems Causing Disunity, 3:1-21
   A. Paul's righteousness: 3:1-16
     1. Not of the law but Christ, 3:1-11
     2. Not yet at stage of perfection, 3:12-16
   B. Paul's Example, 3:17-21

IV. Exhortations Which Will Lead to Unity, 4:1-20
   A. Introductory statement, 4:1
   B. Settlement of differences between women in the church, 4:2, 3
   C. Rejoicing, prayer, and the resultant peace of God, 4:4-7
   D. Controlled thought life, 4:8,9

V. Thanksgiving for Their Gift: A Representation of Their Unified Action, 4:10-20

Conclusion: Greetings from All to All, 4:21-23
   A. Greetings
   B. Benediction

CHAPTER IV

THE ANALYTICAL METHOD

The term *analysis* may be generally defined as a separation of anything into constituent parts or elements, or an examination of anything in its separate parts, as for instance the consideration of the words which compose a sentence or the various propositions which enter into an argument. As related to Scripture, analysis is a detailed study of a book in order to ascertain its message in all its ramifications; as such it is the direct opposite of synthesis, which attempts to look at the book as a whole and to determine its message in general.

In the development of this method there first must be grammatical analysis in which a study is made paragraph by paragraph with determination to discover the principal sentences and to note the grouping around them of subordinate sentences and clauses and the inter-relationships of these. Such a procedure is especially necessary in studying the Pauline epistles, in which the Apostle's constant deviations put the reader in danger of missing the main point of a passage under consideration. In reading a passage of Scripture hastily, it is easy to gain an erroneous impression as to its main theme. A grammatical diagram of the passage might demonstrate that what was considered to be the main theme actually appeared in a subordinate clause; it was not therefore the principal teaching at all.

Reference has been made here to the utilization of the paragraph as the unit of study; this must always be the basis of an intelligent study of the Bible. The reader will recall that the use of the paragraph has already been recommended in the first two methods of this book. As pointed out in those chapters, the American Standard Version will provide the student with a very usable study Bible arranged according to paragraphs.

Analysis to many means merely browsing through the text and stopping here and there to study or comment upon various words, phrases, or ideas. But such is not the case. In the first place, there must be an organized plan for any study of the message of the Word; second, there must be grammatical analysis of the text to discover accurately what that message is. The analytical method, then, will begin with a grammatical diagram of the text, will proceed with a careful outline based on the diagram, and will conclude with various observations on the message thus set forth.

Grammatical analysis involves rewriting the text. Main statements, whether assertions, questions, or commands are placed at the left of the paper. Tenney puts the matter briefly and clearly, "Each line contains one main statement and its modifiers, provided that there is not more than one modifier in each class, and provided that the modifier is not of extraordinary length. Subordinate clauses and phrases are indented above or below the lines of the main statement, depending upon whether they precede or follow it in the order of the text."[1] Modifiers are usually written below the words they modify. When the analysis is complete, the main lines of thought become clear, and the problem of outlining is simplified a great deal.

When the reader is ready to start work on the outline, he should place a blank sheet of paper beside the sheet on which the analysis appears. For the most part, statements which begin at the extreme left of the paper will serve as main points, and indented modifiers will become sub-points. In large measure, all that will be required is a restatement of the analyzed lines of Scripture in good outline form[2] and the placing of letters or numerals before them. This having been done, the student is now

[1] Merrill C. Tenney, *Galatians: The Charter of Christian Liberty*, p. 166. It seems impossible to equal the fine work done by Dr. Tenney on the analytical method in his study of Galatians. Nevertheless, the writer finds it necessary to include a treatment of the method here in an effort to introduce all the different methods of Bible study to the reader in one volume.

[2] See Appendix II for a discussion of outlining.

ready to make observations on the text. Usually he will raise many questions about the message of a passage in the process of analyzing it; now is the time to attempt an answer to them. Further, certain words or concepts may recommend themselves to the student as offering opportunities for profitable study. And he can always fall back on the time-honored "honest serving men" which were introduced in Chapter Two: Who? — author, recipients, principals in a story; What? — action, message, commands; When? — time elements; Where? — geographical notations; Why? — reasons behind the action, message, or commands of the text; How? — in what way does the action of the story affect the participants? In what way has the message of the book affected the author, and how should it change the reader? These questions always serve as effective guides to a thorough knowledge of any subject.

DEMONSTRATION OF EXAMPLE

It is not the purpose of this study to develop any extended portion of Scripture but merely to provide a brief example so the student will have some idea of how to go about analysis by himself. The first two paragraphs of Romans 12 (vv. 1-8) have been chosen. Now let us proceed to develop a grammatical arrangement of the text. Since the first part of verse one constitutes an independent clause, we begin it at the extreme left margin. "I beseech you . . . to present your bodies" is the main part of the sentence and is about all that will go on a line. Because the phrase "by the mercies of God" is parenthetical and is located before the infinitive which is necessary to complete the main verb, we shall place it above the line. The next section of the sentence, "a living sacrifice, holy, acceptable to God," tells the manner of presentation; and the concluding clause in the verse, "which is your spiritual service," tells the reason for the presentation of the body. Therefore, these two lines will be indented slightly. The next sentence, which is coextensive with verse two, contains two main clauses; each of these will start at the left margin, and the final and dependent clause must be

indented under the second main clause. Now we are ready to
work on paragraph two.

Again, the first statement does not happen to be a subordinate
clause, so it will begin at the left margin. Sifted from its surrounding elements, the main statement is "For I say . . . to
every man that is among you." Since the clause "through
the grace that was given me" is parenthetical, it should be indented above the line. The next two portions of the sentence
constitute what the Apostle said and are equal in structure;
they will therefore be indented under "say." The last part of
the sentence, beginning with "according," is subordinate to the
third of the independent clauses and will be indented under
it. Verses four through eight really continue what Paul begins
to "say" in verse three, but we shall bring the main statements
of verses four and five to the left margin in keeping with the
principle set forth earlier that main statements should come to
the extreme left, and to avoid confusion with other material
indented under "say." "So we, who are many, are one body in
Christ" is the last major independent statement in the paragraph. "And severally members one of another" is part of the
compound predicate and therefore will be indented under the
previous statement. The first half of verse six further describes
the "we" of verse five and may be safely put on a parallel with
the statement just quoted. Then a further indentation will be
made for the list of gifts noted in verses 6b-8. The resultant
arrangement will look like this:

<pre>
                      by the mercies of God
I beseech you therefore, brethren/. . . to present your bodies
              a living sacrifice, holy, acceptable to God
              which is your spiritual service.
And be not fashioned according to this world:
but be ye transformed by the renewing of your mind,
              that ye may prove what is the good and acceptable and perfect
                                                will of God.
          through the grace that was given me,
For I say/. . . to every man that is among you,
       not to think of himself more highly than he ought to think
       but so to think as to think soberly,
                 according as God hath dealt to each man a measure of faith.
</pre>

For even as we have many members in one body,
    and all the members have not the same office:
so we, who are many, are one body in Christ,
    and severally members one of another.
    And having gifts differing according to the grace that was given to us,
        whether prophecy, let us prophesy
            according to the proportion of our faith;
        or ministry, let us give ourselves to our ministry;
        or he that teacheth, to his teaching;
        or he that exhorteth, to his exhorting:
        he that giveth, let him do it with liberality;
        he that ruleth, with diligence;
        he that showeth mercy, with cheerfulness.

We are now ready to proceed to step two of the analytical method: the outline. Take a blank piece of paper and place it beside the layout just constructed. We might title the first paragraph "The Apostolic Plea." The first phrase, appearing above the line of the initial main statement, gives the basis of the plea: the mercies of God. The three main statements constitute the content of the plea. In paragraph two the plea changes to command. In the former paragraph, the question had been one of spiritual progress, and a wooing approach is made; in the latter the matter of discipline and order in the Christian community was at stake, and Paul resorts to apostolic command to settle a problem. Just as in the first paragraph, a parenthetical expression appearing above the main statement serves as the basis for the command. The rest of the paragraph serves as the content of the command. While there are four independent statements, each of which ordinarily would rate the position of a major sub-point, the writer feels that the first of these statements is an admonition, the second a reminder, and the third and fourth together constitute an illustration — the figure of the body. If this line of reasoning is followed, the outline produced would be as follows.

I. The Apostolic Plea
    A. Basis — the mercies of God
    B. Content
        1. Presentation of bodies
            a. Manner — living sacrifice
            b. Reason — spiritual (reasonable) service

      2. Non-conformity to the world
      3. Transformation by the renewal of the mind
         — Result: the intellect will be true and exact in judging on moral and spiritual questions

II. The Apostolic Command
    A. Basis — grace (authority) given him
    B. Content
      1. Admonition: do not think too highly of self
      2. Reminder: consider that your position in the Christian community is based on God-given faith
      3. Illustration: examine the figure of the body
         a. Human body — many component parts with various functions
         b. Spiritual body — many members in Christ possessing a variety of gifts which are to be exercised
            (1) prophecy
            (2) ministry
            (3) teaching
            (4) exhortation
            (5) giving
            (6) mercy

Now that the textual analysis and outline have been completed, the next logical step is to make observations on the text. It will not be possible to do this, however, because the passage developed is too short to provide an opportunity for extended study of this kind. It is only as an individual analyzes an entire book or a large portion of it that such follow-up study will be most fruitful. The student should have no difficulty with this part of the analytical method because it will be suited to his own intellectual and spiritual curiosity and ability and will, therefore, have no set pattern of procedure or accomplishment.

CHAPTER V

THE CRITICAL METHOD

The word *criticism* has come into disrepute in many conservative circles because it is usually associated with a destructive liberal attitude toward Scripture. But we need not allow ourselves to be robbed of a perfectly good term, because criticism in itself is legitimate and of value in studying the Bible. The word *criticism* merely implies the formation and expression of a judgment or estimate; and the individual who remarks, "Isaiah in chapter 54 says . . ." is engaging in criticism just as much as one who says that the prophet Isaiah did not write chapters 40-66.

There are two types of criticism — lower and higher. The former, known as textual criticism, deals with the text of the Bible with a view to ascertaining its true and original form. In this field, scholars make use of Hebrew and Greek manuscripts, versions, quotations of or allusions to Scripture in the Church Fathers, or anything else which may possibly bear on the text. Since the aim here is to determine the correct text and not to pass judgment on its origin or value, the work of the lower critic is usually quite objective. Higher criticism begins where lower criticism ends. Believing that the correct text has been discovered, the higher critic (also called the historical or literary critic) seeks to discover whether the claims made by the text or about the text are accurate. Are its authorship and date correct? Is its message technically reliable? — these and many more are questions which he raises. It should be obvious to the reader that there is nothing to fear in the utilization of either of these approaches, when they are rightly applied. In fact, if the Bible is what it claims to be and appears to be, we should fear no investigation; for such inquiry will only demonstrate the truth of the Word and prove to be a powerful apologetic.

Since it is the aim of this present work to provide instruction in methods of Bible study for those who may have little formal education or for students who may not have taken courses in the original languages of Scripture, a detailed discussion of lower criticism is omitted; the advanced student may delve into the matter more at length during his seminary training. Rather, attention here will be devoted to higher criticism.

As in previous chapters, the "honest serving men" are brought into play once more:

Who? Not every personality in a book is comprehended in this question; rather, we are interested in who wrote the book and to whom it was written. The establishment of authorship in the last analysis often depends on both internal and external evidence. In some cases internal evidence is rather conclusive; in others it is scant. The student can discover internal evidence for himself; but for external considerations he must rely upon historical and canonical studies of writers in the field of Biblical introduction. With respect to the discovery of internal evidence, three questions or observations may be made:

1. Does the book claim to be written by any certain individual?
2. If so, could this claim be an arbitrary insertion, the result of forgery? Does the book have a personal tone. Are first personal pronouns utilized? Is autobiographical material so inextricably linked to the rest of the text that it is impossible that it was inserted at a time subsequent to the composition of the book?
3. If the name of the author does not appear in the book, the reader should try to discover references which will enable him to determine the author. If it seems impossible to name a likely candidate, he should try to learn the approximate time of writing and then ask himself what important individuals lived during that

time and might therefore be possible authors. Sometimes it is necessary to rely upon tradition in solving
the problem of authorship.

Having determined the authorship of a book, the reader is now
free to proceed to the second *who?* — the reader, or the one to
whom the book was written. Sometimes this is very clear because the book begins with a statement of address, as in I Corinthians 1:2, "unto the church of God which is at Corinth."
At other times the matter is not quite so clear. In I Peter, for
instance, it may be possible to discover the place to which the
book is addressed, but it is more difficult to determine whether
the readers are Jews or Gentiles. In other books there will be
different kinds of problems in this regard: in Galatians there
is controversy over whether the churches are in north or south
Galatia; in Ephesians there is a textual difficulty regarding the
word *Ephesians,* which does not appear in the best manuscripts;
many feel that the book was written to several churches in
Western Asia Minor; in James the reader must decide what is
implied in "the twelve tribes which are scattered abroad."
Frequently there is no direct address anywhere in the book,
and the student finds it necessary to determine the destination
on the basis of the whole approach of a book. This is especially
well illustrated by the Gospel of Matthew, which one decides
is addressed to the Jews because of the emphasis on the King
of Israel, genealogy, the use of the Old Testament, and other
items which bespeak a definite Jewish flavor.

Where? The question here is place of writing. Very few
books are as clear on this matter as I Corinthians, where the indication is given that the book was written at Ephesus (I Cor.
16:8, 19). In some cases, where there seems to be a definite
statement of place of writing, the matter is not always conclusive; witness in this regard the controversy as to whether
Babylon in I Peter 5:13 means Babylon on the Euphrates or is a
symbolical reference to Rome. As the student studies some
books, there will be sufficient evidence to demonstrate the place
of writing. For the most part, however, it will be a problem
which is either too technical or not worth the time necessary
to dig out all the Biblical indications on the matter. It is ad-

vised, therefore, that various reliable helps be utilized in answering this question. A brief bibliography is provided at the end of this chapter.

When? We now turn to the time of writing. It is impossible to answer this question by means of one's own study of the Scripture because chronological references must always be understood in connection with a knowledge of secular and Biblical history. The dating of the Pauline Epistles in large measure depends on how the Epistles are related to the historical development of the Book of Acts. Luke was written before Acts (Acts 1:1); Acts was written just before Paul was released from Roman imprisonment (Acts 28:30). These and many other chronological indications cannot be used independently to determine the date of books but must be utilized as parts of the whole of Biblical chronology. It is best for the average student to depend on reliable sources for the solution to his problems concerning the time of writing of books of the Bible.

Why? We now set ourselves to determine the reason for the writing of the book, or the occasion. Sometimes this is stated near the beginning of a book, shortly after the salutation; such a procedure is observable in Galatians, where the readers are reprimanded for returning to the legal standard; and in I Timothy, where Timothy is given certain admonitions and instructions concerning his conduct. Once in a while the occasion is stated later in the book; sometimes it is woven throughout the book, as in the case of I Corinthians, where various problems and questions are dealt with (7:1; 7:25; 8:1, 4; 12:1; 16:1; 16:12); and at other times the occasion is implied in a book or is discovered in a study of its historical background.

How? The question to be asked here is, How reliable is the text? Is there any evidence or indication that it has ever suffered editorial rearrangement? What critical destructiveness has been levelled against it? Is the book so arranged as to constitute a unity? As was true of some of the other questions, the answers to these questions will require many study aids.

Development of Example

The Book of Philippians will be utilized to provide an example of this method. Read the book carefully to see what it has to say about authorship. The very first verse mentions Paul and Timothy. A further consideration of personal pronouns as found in the book will demonstrate that they are all in the first person singular when reference is made to the writer, and so Timothy has no claim whatever to authorship. Since almost every verse has one or more forms of the first personal pronoun,[1] it could hardly be maintained that evidences of authorship are arbitrary insertions. Further, the autobiographical material is inextricably linked to the rest of the text. With regard to destination, Philippians 1:1 addresses the book to "the saints at Philippi" and there is no indication that this statement is in any way in error.

The second question we asked ourselves related to the "where" of writing. Here again the epistle itself speaks. Philippians 1:13 mentions the palace (AV), or the Praetorian Guard — the personal bodyguard of Caesar (ASV), and 4:22 mentions Caesar's household; obviously Paul is writing from Rome, and the references to "bonds" indicate that he is in prison.

The decision as to the time of writing requires study helps. Scholars differ slightly on the pinpointing of the time of the first Roman imprisonment — placing it in 59-61, 60-62, 61-63, 62-64. Since the present study does not claim to be a critical work, we shall for the sake of brevity locate its writing between 60-64, though the latter date is probably too late.

Another of the questions introduced in our definition of method was, Why was the book written? This matter was discussed at length in the chapter on the synthetic method, so it is not necessary to go into detail here. We simply state, however, that it was written to serve as a thank-you note, to explain Epaphroditus' illness and delay in returning to the Philippians, and to deal with the problem of disunity among them.

The concluding question asks, How reliable is the text? From the standpoint of internal evidence, it must be said that the message of the book proceeds from beginning to end in a logical and orderly manner. There is no indication of textual corruption or editorial rearrangement.

[1] 1:3, 4, 7, 8, 9, 12, 13, 14, 16, 17, 18, 19, 20, 21, 22, 23, 25, 26, 27, 30; 2:2, 12, 16, 17, 18, 19, 20, 22, 23, 24, 25, 27, 28, 30; 3:1, 3, 4, 7, 8, 9, 10, 11, 12, 13, 14, 15, 16, 17, 18, 20; 4:1, 2, 3, 4, 9, 10, 11, 12, 13, 14, 15, 16, 17, 18, 19, 21.

In the foregoing development, it has been possible in large measure to answer the critical questions about Philippians from the text itself. But for many of the books of the Bible it is necessary to rely almost entirely on books in the field of Biblical introduction for a solution to our problems. Sometimes this is necessary because of the thorny nature of the questions; and at other times our Biblical knowledge may not be such as to provide us with ready answers on the basis of internal evidence, so we turn to one who is particularly familiar with these matters. In an effort to provide further help on this method, by way of example, the critical questions of the authorship and date of Judges are discussed here by means of study aids.

There is no statement in the book which definitely names the author, and we are thus dependent upon various other internal considerations. In the first place, Judges 1:21 states that the Jebusites were still in control of Jerusalem at the time of writing; the Jews were not able to take the city until the seventh year of David (II Sam. 5:6-8). If we adopt the chronology of the kings developed by E. R. Thiele, the reign of David would be 1010-970, and his seventh year 1003. This, then, would be the latest possible date for the writing of Judges. Second, we must consider the formula "In those days there was no king in Israel"; this appears in Judges 17:6; 18:1; 19:1; 21:25. In 17:6 and 21:25 there is added the statement that "every man did that which was right in his own eyes." The implication is that the time of the Judges is now over — "those days" could not refer to the time of the writer's own day — and men no longer do that which is right in their own eyes. If the period of the Judges was over about 1050 and if Jerusalem was taken by David in 1003, the book must have been written sometime in that forty-seven year period, probably in the days of Saul. The most important individual in Jewish history at this particular time — one who bridged the gap between the period of the Judges and the monarchy — was Samuel, and he is the likely author on the basis of internal considerations. Also, Jewish tradition names Samuel as the writer.

SUGGESTIONS FOR FURTHER STUDY

A large number of the books of the Bible may be studied profitably by means of the critical method, but some require the use of fewer helps than others. Four such books are I Corinthians, Galatians, Philemon and Colossians. Others will constitute a very worthwhile study if many study aids are used; this list might include Joshua, Ecclesiastes, Proverbs, I and II Samuel, Isaiah, James and Hebrews.

USEFUL BIBLIOGRAPHY FOR THIS METHOD

There are three good conservative introductions to the Old Testament in print at the present time. It is the problem of introduction to deal with the critical questions discussed in this chapter. One of these works, *Old Testament Introduction* by John H. Raven (New York: Fleming H. Revell, 1906), is rather old and does not, therefore, make reference to recent developments in higher criticism; but other aspects of the book make it a valuable asset to one's library. The other two are Edward J. Young, *An Introduction to the Old Testament* (Grand Rapids: Wm. B. Eerdmans Publishing Company, 1949) and Merrill F. Unger, *Introductory Guide to the Old Testament* (Grand Rapids: Zondervan Publishing House, 1951).

In the field of New Testament introduction, there are also three acceptable conservative books in print. John H. Kerr's *Introduction to the Study of the Books of the New Testament* (Revell, 1898) is rather old but still very useful. Two more recent works are Samuel A Cartledge's *A Conservative Introduction to the New Testament* (6th edition, Zondervan, 1951) and *Introduction to the New Testament* by Henry C. Thiessen (Eerdmans, 1943).

Of course many apologetical works which bear in greater or lesser measure on some of the critical questions as they are related to individual books of the Bible might be suggested here; but it is our present aim to list a restricted number so that any individual of moderate means might purchase them for his library, and it is the desire of the writer to provide titles which will serve as a compact and basic tool kit for use in this method. Four other works should be mentioned, however. Two of these concern themselves specifically with the Pauline Epistles: Frank J. Goodwin, *A Harmony of the Life of St. Paul* (Grand Rapids: Baker Book House), and Conybeare and Howson: *The Life and Epistles of St. Paul* (Eerdmans). The third, Joseph P. Free: *Archaeology and Bible History* (Wheaton Illinois: Van Kampen Press, 1950), provides much helpful material generally related to critical questions. The last, though a survey, includes a great deal of material from the field of introduction; this is Merrill C. Tenney's *The New Testament: An Historical and Analytical Survey* (Eerdmans, 1954).

CHAPTER VI

THE BIOGRAPHICAL METHOD

"Elias [Elijah] was a man subject to like passions as we are . . ." (James 5:17, AV), and for that reason we enjoy studying his life to find there principles to guide our own Christian walk. But Elijah was not the only Biblical character who was human. We must never fall consciously or subconsciously into the attitude that the people of the Bible were superhuman. On the contrary, they were very normal individuals with the same hopes, fears, sins, and capacity for the power of God that we possess; that is why God permitted their names and biographies to be recorded and preserved through the ages. It behooves us, therefore, to devote a great deal of attention to the people of the Bible.

Not only does Biblical biography provide profitable spiritual instruction for the believer, but it presents to him a very worthwhile manner of propagating Christian truth. Since everyone is interested in people and life and living things, educators have used the biographical method of teaching history, literature, and other courses with great success. The same method can be used effectively in teaching spiritual truth.

The biographical method may be studied factually as biographical narrative, homiletically as narrative or character exposition, and polemically or apologetically as biographical argument. It is the purpose of this chapter to deal briefly with all three.

BIOGRAPHICAL NARRATIVE

In the biographical narrative, the aim is simply to learn the biographical facts concerning a Biblical personality, as those details are revealed either in a single book or in all of Scripture. When the student is studying bookwise, it may be desirable for him to confine the investigation of an individual to that particular book in an effort to see the relationship of his life to the message of the text. At other times it will be necessary to uncover all facts concerning an individual. The following simple outline should serve as a handy guide for the development of this method. Obviously, all of the points will not be revealed in a study of every Biblical biography.

   I. Birth and Early Life
      A. Parentage
      B. Place and circumstances of birth
      C. Early training and/or experiences
  II. Conversion Experience and Call to a Specific Task
 III. Ministry for the Lord
      A. Nature of it
      B. Reactions of others to it
 IV. Character Evaluation
      A. Good
      B. Bad
   V. Relationships With Others
  VI. Death and Comments About It
 VII. Reason for the Inclusion of These Facts in the Text

Example of method. Now, by way of example, a study of Paul in the book of II Corinthians, and a consideration of Timothy as all Scriptural references speak of him will be attempted. This will demonstrate the development of both aspects of biographical narrative.

Let us start with the book of II Corinthians. Read the book carefully, jotting down all biographical references as you read. Later, organization and outline will be facilitated if small pieces of note paper are used for each item. Then when the outline is attempted, all that has to be done is the shuffling of these sheets until an effective arrangement is developed, and outline points can then be assigned. The tabulation would include the following:

     1:1 — Paul, an apostle
     1:4, 5 — sufferings for Christ

1:8 ff. — persecution almost to death in Asia but raised up by God

1:11 — received a gift from them

1:12 — bore a good testimony

1:15-22 — change of plans about visiting them was not due to fickleness

1:22, 23 — evidence of conversion

2:1 ff. — attitude of reproof and tender compassion

3:5 — looked to God for sufficiency

3:6 — minister of new covenant

4:2 — upright in daily walk

4:5 — we preach Christ, not ourselves

4:6 — light shined in our hearts — conversion experience

4:10 — experienced constant crucifixion with Christ

4:16 — conscious of physical decline

5:2 ff. — looking forward to the future life

5:5 — evidence of conversion

5:9, 10 — passion to be acceptable to the Lord and conscious of coming judgment

5:11 — fear of the Lord prompts preaching to men

5:14 — constrained by the love of Christ

5:18 — conversion; ministry of reconciliation given to us

5:20 — ambassador for Christ

6:3 — concern lest he be a stumbling block

6:4-11 — fatherly care of and interest in the Corinthians

7:2 — clean and honest record in the ministry

7:9 — does not gloat over wrongdoing of others

7:6; 8:6, 23 — Paul aided by Titus in Macedonian ministry

8:7, 10 ff. — firm in his dealings with the church relative to the collection

10:1, 10 — weak in body and held in contempt

10:8 — possesses authority from God

10:16 — missionary zeal

11:2-4 — concern for Corinthian believers; responsible for founding the church there

11:6 — simple or rude in speech

11:8, 9; 12:13 — Corinthians did not support him while he ministered there

11:22 — Hebrew parentage
11:23-28, 32, 33 — sufferings in the ministry
12:1-8 — caught up into heaven
12:12 — wrought signs of an apostle
12:14; 13:1 — about to pay them a third visit
12:21 — concern for Corinthian believers
13:2, 10 — apostolic authority

Now that we have a reasonably complete list of biographical fact and implication concerning the apostle Paul, the task remains to organize it according to the outline given for this method. The completed product will look something like this.

I. Parentage — Hebrew, 11:22
II. Conversion Experience—evidenced by 1:22, 23; 4:6; 5:5, 18
III. Call to a Specific Task
    A. Apostle, 1:1
       1. Saw the Lord, 12:1ff.
       2. Wrought signs of an apostle, 12:12
       3. Possessed authority, 10:18; 13:10
    B. Ambassador, 5:20
    C. Minister of a new covenant, 3:6
IV. Characteristics or Personal Qualities
    A. Upright in daily walk, 4:2
    B. Simple in speech, 11:6
    C. Humble of spirit, 12:6
    D. Not fickle, 1:15-22
    E. Loving in nature, 2:4; 5:14
    F. Desire for acceptability before God in light of coming judgment, 5:9, 10
    G. Not gleeful over troubles of others, 7:9
    H. Weak of body, 10:10
V. Relationships With Others
    A. Colored by apostleship — firm in dealing with the Corinthian Church, 8:7, 10; 13:2
    B. Accompanied by Timothy and Silvanus in ministering to the Corinthians, 1:19
    C. Associated with Timothy in sending greeting to them, 1:1
    D. Presented with the Philippian gift by Titus, 7:6

VI. Ministry
  A. Characterized by missionary zeal, 10:16
  B. Accompanied by thorn in the flesh, 12:7
  C. Continued in spite of sufferings
    1. Trouble in Asia, 1:8
    2. General physical sufferings, 11:23-33; 1:4, 5
    3. Spiritual sufferings, 4:8ff.
  D. Prompted by
    1. Fear of the Lord, 5:11
    2. Love of Christ, 5:14
  E. Related to the Corinthians
    1. Founded the church there, 11:2-4
    2. Was not supported by them while at Corinth, 11:9; 12:13
    3. Aided by Timothy and Silvanus in work there, 1:19
    4. Possibly presented gift by them after he left them, 1:11
    5. Concerned for them, 12:21; 6:4-11
    6. Planned to make a third trip to them, 12:14; 13:1
  F. Possessed of clean and honest record in the ministry, 1:12; 7:2

VII. Reasons for Including This Biographical Material
  A. To vindicate apostleship
  B. To correct errors in the church
  C. To clear up misconceptions concerning him
  D. To urge to greater service to the Lord
  E. To demonstrate how to live with suffering
  F. To point out sources of spiritual and physical strength

In a complete study of a Biblical character, an analytical concordance is indispensable.[1] Find all of the passages which

[1] Many Bible students possess an abridged Bible concordance by Alexander Cruden, but effective Bible study can best be accomplished with the help of an unabridged concordance. Both those by James Strong and Robert Young are good for the King James Version; M. C. Hazard has produced an unabridged concordance for the American Standard Version.

refer to the character selected — Timothy — and jot down the significant contribution of each. A list similar to the one developed earlier in this chapter will be the result. Then organize the material according to the outline that has been furnished (or one of your own choosing). It seems unnecessary to record all the laboratory work on the person of Timothy here as we did in the case of the study of Paul in II Corinthians; only the completed outline is delineated.

I. Birth and Early Life
    A. Parentage, II Timothy 1:5; Acts 16:1
        1. Mother — Eunice — a Jewess
        2. Father — a Greek
        3. Grandmother — Lois
        4. Mother and grandmother — women of faith
    B. Place of birth — perhaps Asia Minor: Lystra or Iconium
    C. Early training and experiences
        1. Knew Scripture from a babe, II Timothy 3:15
        2. Perhaps made profession very early in life; disciple in Acts 16:1
        3. Circumcised by Paul, Acts 16:3

II. Conversion Experience or Call to a Specific Task
    A. Was a believer
        1. Called unto eternal life, I Timothy 6:12
        2. Possessed unfeigned faith, II Timothy 1:5
        3. Called "our brother," Philemon 1; Colossians 1:1
        4. Called a "disciple," Acts 16:1
        5. Called a "servant of Jesus Christ," Philippians 1:1
    B. Call to ministry — ordained by Paul and the elders, I Timothy 4:14; II Timothy 1:6

III. Ministry for the Lord
    A. Had a good reputation as a disciple before Paul chose him, Acts 16:2
    B. Discovered by Paul at Lystra on second missionary journey, Acts 16:1
    C. Traveled with Paul on remainder of second missionary journey, Acts 16, 17
    D. Traveled with Paul on third missionary journey, Acts 19:22; 20:4

THE BIOGRAPHICAL METHOD

53

E. Accompanied Paul when several epistles were written, Philemon 1; Philippians 1:1; Colossians 1:1; I Thessalonians 1:1; II Thessalonians 1:1; Romans 16:21; II Corinthians 1:1

F. Pastored the church at Ephesus when I and II Timothy were written — apparently quite young at the time, I Timothy 1:3; 4:12; II Timothy 3:22

IV. Character
  A. Dependable — Paul had complete faith in him, I Corinthians 15:10, 11
  B. Full of faith, II Timothy 1:5
  C. Man of God, I Timothy 6:11
  D. Upright, without reproach
    1. Has a good testimony in general, I Timothy 6:12
    2. Well spoken of by brethren at Lystra and Iconium, Acts 16:2

V. Relationships With Others
  A. With Christians at home — well spoken of, Acts 16:2
  B. With Paul
    1. Child in the faith, I Timothy 1:18; 2:2
    2. Faithful in carrying out responsibilities
  C. With yet others on the missionary journeys — no sign of friction

VI. Why Included
  A. Happens to be with Paul when several books are written
  B. Epistles to Timothy are instructions for the church at Ephesus against false teachings and for edification; they are a pattern for pastoral care for centuries to come
  C. To provide an example of a good Christian minister

BIOGRAPHICAL EXPOSITION

A successfully developed biographical narrative provides one with facts concerning a Biblical personality; biographical exposition is reorganization of the same material in such a way that it will be possible to preach it.[2] Of course, the ap-

---

[2] See Appendix III for helpful material on homiletics.

proach is useful for any type of public ministry and is not in the least limited to pulpit oration. Furthermore, this method of Bible study is quite devotional in nature and therefore probably more appealing than biographical narrative. Most homiletics teachers combine all preaching of the lives of Biblical personalities under the heading "biographical exposition," but the writer prefers to divide the field into narrative and character exposition.

In biographical-narrative exposition, the entire span of a man's life is considered, with emphasis on God's dealings with him in the various events and developments of his life, as those dealings relate to him personally or to the history of a group or nation. The theme in this type is not so much the spiritual life of an individual as it is God's care for His own or the preservation of God's chosen people. Biographical-narrative exposition emphasizes events in the person's life, whereas character exposition emphasizes the qualities of an individual and only brings in events to illustrate the message. Character exposition deals more definitely with the character of a man and may in this respect involve only a single story relating to the man. Scripture provides enough material on some Biblical characters to permit either approach, but for many of them we are limited to one method of study.

Biographical-narrative exposition. Probably the best way to outline the life of a man from this standpoint is to look for climactic points which can serve as dividing lines. Joseph is a good illustration of how this may be done. The story of his life quite conveniently falls into three divisions: early life and rejection; servitude and imprisonment; exaltation and reconciliation with his brethren. Another person whose life span divides easily into three periods is Moses; we shall use him as an example of this type of study.

We readily discover that Moses spent forty years in the court of Egypt; forty years in the wilderness; and forty years as leader of his people. As intimated at the beginning of the discussion of biographical exposition, the spade work for this type of study is the same as for biographical narrative: find all the facts relative to an individual by means of a concordance and a careful reading of the Bible. The next step is to outline this material in relation to the time periods established. Our finished product will look something like this.

MOSES — GOD'S GREAT EMANCIPATOR

I. Birth to Banishment
  A. Birth
    1. Parental care
    2. Parental faith
    3. Divine intervention
  B. Training, Acts 7:22
  C. Identification with his people — avenges a Hebrew killed by an Egyptian
  D. Banishment, Acts 7:23
II. Banishment to Burning Bush
  A. Escape from Egypt — God's preservation
  B. Experiences as keeper of sheep
    Note: value of such experiences in preparing him to lead Israelites through area where he spent second forty years of his life
  C. Call of God — to deliver kinsmen from slavery
    Note: decision to do God's will may bring home problems, Exodus 4:25; 18:1ff.
III. Burning Bush to Burial
  A. Experiences with Pharaoh
  B. Journey to Sinai — miraculous provision
    1. Red Sea divided
    2. Water made sweet
    3. Manna and quails provided
    4. Water gushes from rock
    5. Amalekites defeated
  C. Sinai encampment — divine revelation
    1. Law given
    2. People judged
    3. Moses intercedes
    4. Tabernacle set up

D. Journey from Sinai to Nebo — divine judgment and victory
   1. Fire in the midst
   2. Plague of quails
   3. Leprosy on Miriam
   4. Judgment for lack of faith — condemned to wandering
   5. Moses' sin and judgment
   6. Plague of serpents
   7. Victory over King Arad
   8. Victory over Sihon and Og
E. Burial at the hands of God[3]

Character exposition. The first stage of development in character exposition is the same as for the other types mentioned in this chapter. This method lends itself to a greater variety in organization, however. At least five types of procedure may be suggested. The first asks three questions: What was he? What made him that way? What was the result of what he became? The second details in a two-point outline (1) the environment and influences brought to bear on an individual and (2) the results of them. In the third approach, an effort is made to search out the individual's dominant personal traits; then his personality traits which are outstandingly worth admiring are selected, and incidents from his life or work which will bring these before the audience are related. Lastly, one should show how these traits influenced the individual's decisions, impressed others, or enabled him to overcome obstacles. Another way to develop this study is to pick out a few of the person's outstanding accomplishments; then to demonstrate the effects or significance of these accomplishments; and thirdly, to demonstrate the factors which made the accomplishments possible. The fifth method seeks to demonstrate the influence a man has upon the lives of his fellow men or on the course of events, and then shows how the hearer may improve his influence on society. Of course,

---

[3] A glance at this outline will demonstrate that this is too much material to cover in one sermon; either certain points could be emphasized or a series of three messages could be preached on the subject.

there are many other recommendations that could be made to the student of character exposition; Wilbur M. Smith lists fifteen points in his suggested development of this type of Bible study.

"I. Collect all the material which the Bible contains concerning the one character about to be studied. In doing so, be sure that you are not gathering material for two or more different persons of the same name, e.g., there are thirty characters in the Old Testament by the name of Zechariah, there are fifteen characters in the Old Testament by the name of Jonathan, and there are twenty characters by the name of Nathan. . . .

"II. Carefully study the ancestry of each character, and especially the characteristics of the parents, if they are known.

"III. Attempt to estimate the advantages in training which the subject of your study had during the early days of his or her youth.

"IV. Carefully attempt to determine the work which your character accomplished.

"V. What was the great crisis in this person's life, and how did he meet it?

"VI. What traits of character does this person display throughout his life?

"VII. What friendships did the man have — were they noble or ignoble; did they help him or hinder him in his life work?

"VIII. Determine, as far as possible, the influence this particular character had upon others, upon the nation, upon the history of religion.

"IX. What growth does the character of this person show?

"X. Carefully determine the religious experiences of the character you are studying — his prayer life, faith in God, service for God, knowledge of the Scriptures, courage in testimony, and his attitude in worship.

"XI. What faults and shortcomings are revealed?

"XII. What do you think was the great sin in any one character's life, if there was one? What was the nature of the sin? What were the steps leading up to the sin? What effect did this sin have upon this person's future?

"XIII. What do you find to be the character and influence of this person's children?

"XIV. In what way do you think the character you are studying is a type or anti-type of Christ?

"XV. What is the one great lesson in this person's life for you?"[4]

Only one example of character exposition is attempted here, and this follows the first of the five types of approach described earlier. The individual to be studied is Absalom. After all the Biblical information concerning Absalom is gathered with the help of a concordance, we may outline it briefly as follows.

I. His Person
   A. Attractive qualities
      1. Charming beauty, II Samuel 14:25
      2. Leadership ability, II Samuel 15:13ff.
      3. Parentage — son of a king
   B. Unattractive features
      1. Selfish
      2. Vain, II Samuel 15:4ff.
      3. Disloyal, II Samuel 15:1ff.
      4. Hate, II Samuel 13:22

II. Home background
   A. Godless mother—Maacah the Geshurite, II Samuel 3:3
   B. Pre-occupied father — many battles and responsibilities of state
   C. Environment of corruption, II Samuel 16:21
   D. Neglect of personal relationship to God
   E. Incomplete forgiveness on the part of David — allowed Absalom to live in Jerusalem two years without seeing him, II Samuel 14:28

III. Fruits of his character
   A. Murder of Amnon, with consequent three-year exile and two years of broken fellowship with David
   B. Strife to nation, II Samuel 15ff.
   C. Premature death, II Samuel 18:15
   D. Broke heart of his father, II Samuel 15:30; 18:33

[4] Wilbur M. Smith, *Profitable Bible Study* (Boston: W. A. Wilde Company, 1953), pp. 44-46.

E. Brought grief to various individuals, e.g., Joab's field was burned, II Samuel 14:30

F. Handed down a bad name, II Samuel 18:18

G. Probably sent his own soul to eternal punishment

BIOGRAPHICAL ARGUMENT

One more type of biographical study falls within the province of this chapter: biographical argument. This may be defined as the utilization of biographical fact to demonstrate the validity of the message one preaches or to add weight to certain facets of truth he is trying to proclaim. It is difficult to set forth any definite procedure for the study of this method; the approach varies in each place that it is used. The student should locate passages where the author uses his own experiences or the biography of another to defend or illustrate doctrinal truth and then organize his outline according to the steps in the argument of the writer. By way of example, Dr. Tenney finds five steps in the biographical argument of the first two chapters of Galatians, where Paul defends the divine origin of his message, his doctrinal agreement with the other apostles, and his apostleship.

"First of all, the autobiographical narrative indicates that he had not espoused the cause of the gospel because of any natural inclination toward it. . . .

"Secondly, the sudden change of his faith was the direct result of divine intervention. . . .

"Thirdly, his message was not taken over from new contacts or from a new environment. . . .

"Paul did not want his independence to be construed as heresy or as radical digression from the common core of apostolic teaching.

"The apparent disagreement between Paul and the apostles arose over a question of consistency in behavior rather than in theology."[5]

SUGGESTIONS FOR FURTHER STUDY

Biographical argument is probably the least usable of the biographical methods detailed in this chapter because it is utilized so infrequently. It does, however, figure in several books

[5] Merrill C. Tenney, *Galatians: The Charter of Christian Liberty*, pp. 84, 85.

of the Bible. Paul uses it to some extent in Philippians and I and II Corinthians, and Jesus uses it occasionally in the Gospels. There is abundant opportunity to use character exposition. Probably the largest single group of individuals that could be studied profitably in this way is the kings of Israel and Judah. For many of them, not too much is left to the imagination because God condemns or commends their practices. Several which may be studied to advantage are Rehoboam, Jeroboam, Ahab, Jehoshaphat, Jehoram, Jehu, Josiah and Hezekiah.[6] A host of individuals among the prophets, patriarchs, disciples, and judges might be added to this list. Biographical narrative exposition is somewhat more limited in scope because fewer individuals are described extensively in Scripture. In addition to the examples already named for this type, we might mention Lot, Abraham, Isaac, Jacob, Samuel, David, Daniel and Paul. Simple biographical narrative can be applied to almost any Biblical personality because all that method seeks to do is discover everything the Scripture has to say about the individual.

HELPFUL BIBLIOGRAPHY

For the most part, the student should avoid books about Biblical characters until he has made a complete study of Biblical facts concerning them with the help of a good concordance. Even the best authors on the subject become speculative at times in an effort to fill in the gaps left in a biography by the Scriptural narrative. If the student makes his own study first, he will readily recognize where this supplementary material has been added and will not confuse the imagination of men with the inspiration of God. Furthermore, a sanctified imagination is of value to every believer; and too much dependence on the imagination of another will prevent his own from maturing. There are, however, a few books in the field that might be mentioned. *The International Standard Bible Encyclopedia* (Grand Rapids: Wm. B. Eerdmans Publishing Co.) is an excellent aid to the rapid accumulation of basic facts about Biblical characters. Every person in the Bible is factually described

---

[6] A valuable aid to the study of Old Testament kings is *A Harmony of Samuel, Kings and Chronicles* by William D. Crockett (Grand Rapids: Baker Book House).

in this set of five volumes. Along this same line, *Harper's Bible Dictionary* by Miller and Miller (New York: Harper & Brothers) and *Smith's Bible Dictionary* by William Smith (Grand Rapids: Zondervan Publishing House) may be noted. The classic interpretative work on Bible character study is Alexander Whyte's *Bible Characters* (Zondervan); this was formerly published in six volumes and is now available in two. A fine series of volumes on individual characters is written by F. B. Meyer. Many of these recently have been reprinted by Zondervan Publishing House. Another valuable Zondervan publication in this field is *Bible Characters* by Moody, Talmage, and Parker; this volume includes eighty-two sermons on major and minor characters of the Bible.

CHAPTER VII

THE HISTORICAL METHOD

It is customary in many of the schools of our nation to study literature from the standpoint of appreciation only; beauty, form, and general content occupy almost all of the attention of the students. Little effort is made to evaluate the place of a literary work in the experience of the author or to show what historical conditions produced the work or what effect the composition may have had on people of that day or subsequent periods of time. While a purely aesthetic approach is of great value, it is the opinion of the writer that the student will gain a much better understanding of literature if these historical questions are brought into the account. The Bible is no exception to this observation. It is true that there is tremendous value in devotionalizing on the contents of the Word, but many passages will have little or no meaning for the believer unless he seeks to understand their historical context and importance.

The historical method may be applied factually to the study of a book or an event; or it may be developed homiletically as narrative exposition. All three are comprehended in the present consideration.

THE STUDY OF A BOOK

A slightly different approach must be taken for each of these three types of historical treatment. When the student is considering an entire book, he may follow four general points.

1. *Setting of the book — its place in the life of the writer or the history of a people.* If the book is one of the Pauline Epistles, we should ask where it fits into Paul's life and ministry. On what missionary journey was it written? Did he ever visit the church? If so, how many times? If a book under consideration was written by some other known author, where does

it fit into his life and ministry? If the name of the author is not known, where does the book fit into the history of the nation of Israel and the nations surrounding it?

2. *Historical narrative represented in the book.* When the book being studied is a Pauline Epistle that deals with a specific church, several items need to be developed: the account of the founding of the church; its composition — whether Jew or Gentile; the place of meeting; special problems facing the church; and the historical events which occasioned this particular letter. In other books, the historical and chronological content or plan of the book might be detailed at this point.

3. *Historical importance of the book.* We are interested now in the importance of the book in history. What special doctrinal contributions does it make to the Hebrew-Christian tradition? If it is a New Testament work, how close to the origin of the Christian Church was it written? What is the history of the book in the Church — has there ever been a struggle over its canonicity?

4. *Textual evidences and inferences of what life was like at the time and in the area comprehended by the book.* What does the text intimate concerning the nature of the life of the people referred to in this book? What can be learned in this regard from other sources? If the reader is considering a Pauline epistle, this is the time to place the church of that epistle in its historical context. Note the nature of Roman society of the first century A. D. Discover what life was like in the town where the church is located, as a result of its industries, religion, or general location. A brief history of the town might be in order. Other books of the Bible, when studied in this way, will require a knowledge of Hebrew, Babylonian, Assyrian, Egyptian, Canaanite, or Persian history and society.

HISTORICAL EVENT

The plan for developing an historical event is quite different from that just outlined. (1) In the first place, survey the event; discover the general movement of the event; characterize the persons involved; note the amount of time consumed. (2) Place the event in the book as a whole. Why is it where it is? What does it contribute to the progress of the book as a whole? (3) Place the event chronologically in the life of an individual or nation. (4) What caused the event or what led up to it? (5) What were the effects of it to persons involved, to posterity, to the history of the nation, movement, town, or area, and in the doctrinal or ideological development of the Hebrew-Christian tradition?

NARRATIVE EXPOSITION

Narrative exposition involves specific incidents more often than whole books, but short books may be treated effectively in this way. By way of parenthesis, let it be said that narrative exposition is not merely the telling of a story; it is the organization of the Biblical material at the disposal of the speaker in such a way as to present the message of the event in a compelling way. Several approaches could be taken. In the first place, one might wish to divide the story into scenes as he would a drama and emphasize the main point of each. In the second place, observations could be made concerning each character or group of characters in the story. Third, a consideration of the various circumstances of one person in the story could serve as the basis of organization, the lesser important characters being thrown into the background. Last, it is often effective to tell the story quickly in order to get it before the hearer, then to point out the teachings which are to be derived from the story, and finally to apply the teachings to the hearts of the hearers. Various modifications and combinations of these general plans will also prove useful in this type of study.

DEVELOPMENT OF EXAMPLE
The Study of a Book

The study of I Corinthians is chosen as an example of the historical method as applied to a whole book. Paul paid his first visit to Corinth after the Mars Hill experience at Athens (Acts 18:1) and ministered there for a year and six months (Acts 18:11), after which he began the trip back to Palestine and Syria. On the third journey, near the end of a three-year stay in Ephesus, Paul found it necessary to visit the Macedonian churches again and spent three months in the process (Acts 20:1-6). That he visited Corinth during this journey seems obvious on the basis of such verses as II Corinthians 2:1; 12:14, 21; 13:1, 2. Evidently I Corinthians was written from Ephesus (I Cor. 16: 8, 9, 19) while Paul was on the third journey. Composition probably dates to the latter half of his three-year stay there because during the first part of the Ephesus sojourn Apollos was ministering in Corinth, and it was Apollos' ministry which in large measure called forth the writing of the letter.

Our investigation now centers on the historical account of the founding of the church and attendant circumstances. The account of the establishment of the Corinthian church is recorded in Acts 18:1-18. Upon arrival in Corinth, Paul began his ministry in the synagogue, as was his custom. When the Jews rejected him, he turned to the Gentiles and many of them believed, including Crispus, the chief ruler of the synagogue. At this point the Jews stirred up some trouble and brought Paul before Gallio, the Roman official of the city. After his acquittal on this count, Paul continued his ministry there for a time and then left for Palestine. With regard to the question concerning the composition of the church, it becomes quite obvious that while there were a few Jews in the congregation (note Crispus), most of the believers were Gentiles. Paul's main ministry there was to Gentiles and the nature of some of the problems which arose in the Corinthian church were peculiar to Gentiles. For instance, the issue of eating meats offered to idols was primarily a Gentile matter. The historical occasion for the writing of the book is the existence of factional disputes and other problems in the Corinthian church as reported to Paul through the household of Chloe (I Cor. 1:11), Apollos (I Cor. 16:12), Stephanas, Fortunatus, and Achaicus (I Cor. 16:17), and a letter sent by the church (I Cor. 7:1).

The book is historically important first of all for its doctrinal contribution to the Hebrew-Christian tradition. It is unique in its teachings about the baptism and indwelling of the Holy Spirit, the condition one should be in before partaking of the

Lord's Supper, control of the use of spiritual gifts, saints going to law with each other, carnality, and marriage. Here, too, are classic passages on love and the resurrection.

As far as the history of the book in the Church is concerned, all that need be said is that the evidence for its existence and recognition is abundant and continuous. But it might be added that Clement of Rome, as early as 95 A.D., makes reference to it in his *Epistle to the Corinthians;* Marcion included it in his heretical canon (c. 140); it appears in the Muratori Canon (c. 160); and it is among the Pauline Epistles which circulated as a group by the end of the second century.

Last, we endeavor to discover various items in the book which relate to the historical and social context of that day. This is a vast subject — one which would require an entire volume if developed in all of its ramifications; therefore, a few examples must suffice here. The book well pictures the life and problems of a first century church in the midst of a pagan community. There were the questions of meat offered to idols and the lack of sanctity of sex and the general immorality of the populace. The religious prostitution carried on by hundreds of priestesses in the service of Aphrodite, whose temple was located on the acropolis at Corinth, and the lack of inhibition characteristic of the transient population of Corinth's great trading centers and industrial enterprises would hardly provide a context conducive to a high moral standard on the part of the Christians there. Another indication of historical context is given in the fact that it was the oratorical ability of Apollos which was in large measure responsible for the factional dispute raging in the church. The Greeks were proud of their oratorical ability. Also it should be noted that Corinth was famous for the great Isthmian games which were held every two years near the city. Universal in appeal, they attracted athletes and visitors from all over Greece. It is to these that Paul makes reference in I Corinthians 9:24-27.

A Study of an Event

A study of Sennacherib's effort to take Jerusalem serves as a good example of the historical method as related to an event. The story is recorded in II Kings 18:13-19:37; II Chronicles

32:1-21; and Isaiah 36:1-37:38. The narrative may be briefly told. Sennacherib led an army into Judah. Hezekiah, terrified, offered to pay tribute in an effort to buy him off. After Hezekiah raised the required amount, Sennacherib sent three of his officers and a large body of troops to Jerusalem to attempt a conquest of the capital. Rab-shakeh, seemingly the Assyrian officer in charge, tried to soften up Jewish resistance by leading a propaganda barrage against the defenders of the walls. The report was brought to King Hezekiah, who repaired to the temple in great consternation and sent a delegation to Isaiah for advice. Isaiah then predicted that harm would befall Sennacherib and that he would return to his own land, where he would be slain. Rab-shakeh relayed this message to Sennacherib, then encamped near Libnah, and the king sent a sabre-rattling letter to Hezekiah. The Hebrew king again refused to be cowed and sought further help from the Lord. The Lord sent Isaiah with a message of comfort to Hezekiah, and the prophet predicted divine deliverance for Jerusalem. That night 185,000 Assyrian troops died of plague, and Sennacherib returned to his homeland, where eventually he was slain by his sons while he was at worship.

These events must have consumed several days or weeks in the fourteenth year of Hezekiah. If the dates of his reign are 716-687, the fourteenth year probably would be 702, some twenty years after the fall of Samaria to Assyria. Sennacherib's invasion of Judea is a logical outcome of the plea of the wicked King Ahaz (father of Hezekiah), who asked the intervention of Assyria in Palestinian affairs so that Judah might be protected; he sought not the help of the Lord.

The last of our list of questions given as a guide for the study of this method inquires about the effects of the event. It was important to persons involved because it meant a serious setback to the plans of Sennacherib for world conquest and a curse upon his life.[1] To Hezekiah it meant a triumph of

---

[1] The reader might get the idea that Sennacherib was killed immediately on return to Nineveh, but the curse was not fulfilled until 681 B.C., about twenty years later. The aim of Scripture was to demonstrate the fulfillment of prophecy, not to record all the subsequent events of the life of Sennacherib.

faith and perpetuation of his kingly position. To Jerusalem it meant the alleviation of the siege and continued freedom instead of slavery or death. To the nation it meant continued perpetuity. Religiously it demonstrates the faithfulness of God and His response to the prayer of faith.

NARRATIVE EXPOSITION

We shall now attempt to provide examples of narrative exposition. Mark 6:45-52 is chosen for illustration of this type of Bible study. A brief outline of the story according to the initially suggested plan — division into scenes — is given first.

I. The Aftermath
   A. The Savior's desire to be alone
   B. The disciples' obedience

II. The Situation on the Sea
   A. The disciples' plight
   B. The Master's concern
   C. The disciples' lack of perception
   D. The Master's omnipotence

Next are listed two outlines composed by students who have taken this course. The first details the action in relation to the main character, and the second develops the narrative according to the fourth plan given earlier in the chapter. There the story is told quickly; the typical significance is noted; and the teaching of the story is applied.

JESUS AND THE —

I. Multitude (of people)
   A. Satisfied
   B. Sent away

II. Mountain (of prayer)
   A. Passion
   B. Prayer

III. Misgiving (of disciples)
   A. Wind
   B. Walk

IV.   Miracle (of Jesus)
    A.   Peace
    B.   Presence
 V.   Misunderstanding (of disciples)
    A.   Surprise
    B.   Superficiality

—Norman E. Pyle

FAITH AND FEAR

 I.   The Story — the fearful disciples crossing the stormy sea
    A.   Preceding event — feeding of the five thousand
    B.   Christ's urgency for prayer
        1.   He sends the disciples on in the boat before Him
        2.   He sends the multitude away
        3.   He departs into the mountain to pray
    C.   The distressed disciples
        1.   The stormy night at sea without Jesus
        2.   Rowing against the wind
        3.   Jesus supposed to be a ghost
    D.   The calming Savior
        1.   He calms the disciples
        2.   He calms the storm
    E.   The spiritual short-sightedness of the disciples
        1.   They forgot the former miracle
        2.   Their heart was hardened
II.   Teaching of the Story
    A.   Jesus' emphasis on the spiritual
        1.   His urgency for prayer even after the victorious miracle
        2.   His words of comfort to the fearful disciples
    B.   The disciples' lack of faith and spiritual understanding
        1.   In the midst of their work in the storm:
            a.   They forgot that the miracle-working Christ had sent them
            b.   They didn't recognize Jesus when He came to them
        2.   They failed to receive the lesson from the feeding

of the five thousand and transfer its teaching to
another situation

III. Typical Significance of the Story
   A. We should refuse to let our work and distressing con-
ditions overshadow the call of God and presence of
Christ
   B. Christ can calm the inner fears and conflicts of man
   C. Spiritual truths can and should be transferred to every-
day conditions and experiences of life
—Charles Ford

The last outline to be provided in the study of the Mark
passage is something of a variation of the second and fourth
suggested procedures of narrative exposition.

CHRIST — THE ONE THROUGH WHOM WE CAN MEET ALL THE
STORMS OF LIFE

I. The Scene
   A. Dismissal of assembled people
      1. Disciples dismissed
      2. Multitude dismissed
      3. Christ ascends into a mountain
   B. Situation on the sea
      1. Toiling in rowing
      2. Christ's awareness of it
   C. Presence of Jesus with the disciples
      1. Christ appearing
      2. Disciples' reaction
      3. Calming of storm
      4. Completed journey

II. The Disciples
   A. They were obeying the Lord
   B. They were in trouble while obeying the Lord
   C. They were delivered out of their trouble

III. Jesus
   A. Desire for communion
      1. Dismissal of the gathering
      2. Direction of the disciples

   B. Knowledge of situation on the sea
       1. Troubled disciples
       2. Vision of Christ
       3. Action of Christ — came unto them
   C. Presence with His disciples
       1. Value — depended upon their recognition of Him
       2. Presence with them — was a guarantee against fear
           and assurance of calm

A further illustration of the fourth type of narrative exposition may be seen in the following outline of John 5:1-9.

HUMAN IMPOTENCE AND DIVINE POWER

  I. The Picture of the Story — scene at the pool
      A. Healing waters
      B. People
      C. Individual selected
      D. Question and answer
      E. Command and response
 II. Typical Significance of the Story
      A. Physical and spiritual condition of the man (of men)
      B. Healing wrought by Christ (saving power)
III. The Subject of the Story
      A. Man's condition
          1. Result of sin
          2. Recognition of helplessness
      B. Man's heartfelt desire for healing
      C. Man's healing — by divine action

SUGGESTIONS FOR FURTHER STUDY

Almost any of the Pauline Epistles provide fruitful studies of the historical method as applied to a book, but the Pastoral Letters (I, II Timothy, and Titus) are more personal in nature and do not lend themselves to this type as well as letters to the young churches. Acts, of course, must be considered in conjunction with the Pauline Epistles. A few Old Testament books, as Joshua, Ruth, Ezra, and Nehemiah, may also be considered in this way. The Gospels, along with such books as Judges, Kings, Chronicles, and portions of Genesis and Exodus embody so many short narratives that it seems wise to develop them from the standpoint of the study of an historical event as outlined earlier in this chapter. Narrative exposition works effectively with almost any Bible stories of reasonable length, but of special interest will be the miracles of Jesus, escapades of the kings of Israel and Judah, events of the wilderness wanderings of the Children of Israel, and varied experiences and/or miracles of such prophets as Elijah and Elisha.

HELPFUL BIBLIOGRAPHY

Adams, J. M., *Biblical Backgrounds* (Nashville: Broadman Press, 1938).

Cartledge, Samuel A., *A Conservative Introduction to the New Testament* (6th ed.; Grand Rapids: Zondervan Publishing House, 1951).

Fairweather, William, *The Background of the Epistles* (Edinburgh: T. & T. Clark, 1935).

———, *The Background of the Gospel* (4th ed.; Edinburgh: T. & T. Clark, 1926).

Filson, Floyd V., *The New Testament Against Its Environment* (3rd ed.; London: The SCM Press).

Kerr, John H., *An Introduction to the Study of the Books of the New Testament* (New York: Fleming H. Revell Co., 1892).

Miller, Madeleine S., and J. Lane, *Encyclopedia of Bible Life* (New York: Harper & Brothers, 1944).

———, *Harper's Bible Dictionary* (New York: Harper & Brothers, 1952).

The New Schaff-Herzog Encyclopedia of Religious Knowledge (Grand Rapids: Baker Book House, 1949). 13 volumes.

Orr, James, ed., *The International Standard Bible Encyclopaedia* (Grand Rapids: Wm. B. Eerdmans Publishing Co., 1943). 5 volumes.

Ramsay, W. M., *The Cities of St. Paul* (London: Hodder & Stoughton, 1907; reprinted by Baker Book House).

———, *St. Paul the Traveller and the Roman Citizen* (8th ed.; London: Hodder & Stoughton, 1905; reprinted by Baker Book House).

Raven, John Howard, *Old Testament Introduction* (New York: Fleming H. Revell Co., 1906).

The Seventh-day Adventist Bible Commentary (Washington, D.C.: Review and Herald Publishing Association, 1954). 7 volumes. The introductory chapters of each of these volumes are of special value in that they deal with historical and chronological problems of the Bible in the light of the latest discoveries of modern scholarship.

Smith, William, *Smith's Bible Dictionary* (rev. ed.; Grand Rapids: Zondervan Publishing House, 1953).

Tenney, Merrill C., *The New Testament: An Historical and Analytical Survey* (Grand Rapids: Wm. B. Eerdmans Publishing Co., 1954).

Thiessen, Henry C., *Introduction to the New Testament* (Grand Rapids: Wm. B. Eerdmans Publishing Co., 1943).

Unger, Merrill F., *Introductory Guide to the Old Testament* (Grand Rapids: Zondervan Publishing House, 1951).

Wright, G. Ernest, *The Old Testament Against Its Environment* (3rd ed.; London: The SCM Press).

Young, Edward J., *An Introduction to the Old Testament* (Grand Rapids: Wm. B. Eerdmans Publishing Co., 1949).

CHAPTER VIII

THE THEOLOGICAL METHOD

Theology may be simply defined as the science of God — a summary and study of religious truth scientifically arranged. If it is a science, it is more than a mere knowledge of facts; it must include a demonstration of the vital relation of those facts to each other in an integrated system so that if component parts of the whole are accepted, the reception of those parts carries with it assent to the whole. While a development of the physical sciences is based on empirical knowledge, theological science ultimately rests on revelation and therefore must be accepted by faith — though a very effective verification of its factuality is made by the studies of Biblical evidences and by apologetics.

The Bible is not a systematic theology; it is no more a system of theology than nature is a system of chemistry. While the Bible is the source of all theological knowledge, man has the privilege and responsibility of systematizing the truth found therein. It is the purpose of this method to engage in such systematization — not to develop a complete systematic theology with a philosophical discussion of all of the implications as the large sets of theological works attempt to do, but to provide organized studies of certain facets of Biblical knowledge that will profit the believer in his doctrinal investigation of the Word and in his daily walk. The theological method may be defined as the process of searching through an individual book or the Bible as a whole to collect, compare, and organize doctrinal statements and assumptions.

74

Types of Theological Study

The field of geometry is effectively pursued only when certain axioms and postulates are accepted as the basis for mathematical study. Just so, there are numerous theological assumptions which recognizably underlie Biblical study. Our first type of theological study, then, is the consideration of theological assumptions behind the message of a book of the Bible or any part of it. Among the common facts taken for granted in Scripture are the existence of God, the idea that God is interested in men, the power and personality of God, and the inspiration of the Word. In an investigation of this kind, it is necessary first of all to tabulate the basic assumptions of the passage which the student has chosen for development; second, an effort should be made to demonstrate how these assumptions are indispensable to the theological message; and third, careful attention should be given to the references to these assumptions in order to discover what they intimate or specifically state about the main doctrinal message of the text under consideration.

The second type of theological study is probably the most common way of pursuing the theological method — the consideration of the explicit doctrinal teaching of a book. The idea here is not to wring the last bit of doctrinal content from every word of a portion of Scripture but to ascertain its main theological message. This kind of investigation may be applied to an entire book, such as I or II Thessalonians, where the theme of the second coming of Christ pervades the whole of the epistles; or it may be utilized in the study of a doctrinal section of a book, for example: Roman 1-11, Ephesians 1-3, and Philippians 2. As already intimated, we are not interested at this point in theological implication but explicit or clear and definite teaching on a given subject. Probably the best way to get at the doctrinal message of a portion — if it is a long one — is to name the paragraphs and develop a good outline according to the procedure suggested in the discussion of the synthetic method. A short passage could be outlined according to smaller units of thought, in the manner of the analytical method. When the outline is completed, the student will be in possession of the main line of doctrinal content of the text and will be able to trace the turns of thought in that argument.

Yet another approach to theological study of the Bible is achieved by means of subject or topical study. This may be attempted either in the direct or indirect manner. In the former, one word or theological element is considered. Examples of words are *grace, law, love, life, sin,* and *world;* theological elements might include the Holy Spirit in Acts, the person of Christ in a Pauline epistle, and the names of God and their significance. In the indirect type of study, a theme or idea or concept is developed. In this case one gets at the whole of a doctrine indirectly by investigating all of the words related to it. For instance, in an illustration to be provided later, the whole doctrine of temptation is arrived at by means of a study of related terms such as *try, test,* or *prove.* The procedure in either case is the same. Occurrences of terms or materials bearing on a given theme are gathered by means of a concordance or frequent and careful reading and notation. Secondly, terms are defined through close scrutiny of their usage in relation to their context. Then an outline of the study is prepared. Not only will this outline serve the Bible student in his future research but also it will be of great help to the minister in subject exposition (or a topical sermon, according to terminology used by some).

THEOLOGICAL FRAMEWORK

In order to facilitate theological study of the Bible, a brief outline of Biblical theology is furnished at this point. Items in the outline are explained when it is felt necessary. This should aid the student both in inductive and deductive development of theological themes. In induction, scattered inferences relative to a given subject are collected, compiled, and outlined in an effort to formulate general concepts; the outline helps one to see how he may better organize the conclusions to which he has come. For the purposes of deductive investigation, general themes or subjects may be selected from this outline and their assertions amplified and confirmed.

I. Bibliology[1]
   A. The supernatural origin of the Bible
   B. Revelation
   C. Inspiration
   D. Illumination
   E. Canonicity and authority
   F. Interpretation
II. Theology Proper — what may be known of God's triune personality
   A. The attributes of God
      1. Personality
      2. Omniscience
      3. Sensibility
         a. Holiness
         b. Justice
         c. Love
         d. Goodness
         e. Truth
      4. Will
         a. Freedom
         b. Omnipotence
      5. Unity
      6. Infinity
      7. Eternity
      8. Immutability
      9. Omnipresence
      10. Sovereignty
   B. Divine works — discusses subject of sovereignty and election
      1. Creation
      2. Decrees
      3. Preservation
   C. Names of deity
   D. Trinitarianism
      1. Proof of doctrine
      2. God the Father

[1] Adapted from Lewis Sperry Chafer, *Systematic Theology*, (Dallas: Dallas Seminary Press, 1947).

       3. God the Son
         a. His pre-existence
         b. His names
         c. His deity
         d. His incarnation
         e. His humanity
         f. His attributes
         g. His hypostatic union — unity of two natures (divine and human) in one person
       4. God the Holy Spirit
         a. Personality
         b. Deity
         c. Titles
         d. Relationships

III. Angelology
    A. General facts about angels
    B. Satan's evil character
    C. Satan's evil career
    D. Demonology

IV. Anthropology — study of the origin and nature of man
    A. The origin of man
    B. The fall
    C. Sin and the sin nature
    D. Cure for sin

V. Soteriology — the doctrine of salvation
    A. The Savior
       1. His person
         a. Names
         b. Deity
         c. Humanity
         d. Hypostatic union
         e. Attributes
         f. Offices
           (1) Prophet
           (2) Priest
           (3) King

      2. His sufferings
        a. In life
        b. In death
      3. Things accomplished by Christ in sufferings and death
    B. The saving work
      1. Finished work of Christ
      2. Convicting work of Spirit
      3. Terms of salvation
      4. Eternal security

VI. Ecclesiology — study of the doctrine of the Church
    A. The Church as an organism — the Body of Christ
    B. The contrast between Israel and the Church
    C. The Church as an organization — local church
      1. Her doctrine
      2. Her service
      3. Her ordinances
      4. Her order

VII. Eschatology — study of teachings concerning the last things
    A. Prophecy concerning the Church
    B. Prophecy concerning Israel
    C. Prophecy concerning the Messiah
    D. The judgments
    E. The tribulation
    F. The millennium
    G. The eternal state

VIII. Christology — study of the person of Christ
    A. The pre-incarnate Christ
    B. Christ incarnate
      1. Birth and childhood
      2. Baptism
      3. Temptation
      4. Transfiguration
      5. Teachings
      6. Miracles
      7. Sufferings and death

        8. Resurrection

        9. Ascension and Session

    C. Second Advent

    D. Messianic kingdom

  IX. Pneumatology — study of the doctrine of the Holy Spirit

    A. Names

    B. Deity

        1. Divine attributes (see under "attributes of God")

        2. Divine works

    C. Types and symbols

    D. The Holy Spirit in the Old Testament

    E. Ministry in New Testament period

    F. Ministry in present age

        1. Relation to unsaved

           a. Restrain

           b. Convict

      2. Relation to saved

           a. Regenerating

           b. Indwelling

           c. Baptism

           d. Sealing

           e. Filling

           f. General enabling

EXAMPLE OF METHOD

Examples of only the second and third types of theological method are provided here as they will prove more useful to the average student than will the first. A study of Ephesians 1-3 is developed as an example of the second type, in which a consideration of the explicit doctrinal teaching of a book is involved. The main message of Ephesians concerns the Church as the body of Christ, and as such it contrasts with Colossians, which treats the head of that body — Christ. The first half of Ephesians is doctrinal; and the second half is practical, emphasizing the walk of members of the body. As recommended above, we shall start out by naming the paragraphs.

Paragraph	Reference (ASV)	Name
1	1:1, 2	Greetings to the body
2	1:3-14	Blessings for members of the body
3	1:15-23	Prayer for members of the body who are positionally seated in the heavenlies that they may have light to know
4	2:1-10	How we become members of the body
5	2:11-22	Jew and Gentiles are members of one body
6	3:1-13	Paul is minister to the Gentiles, who are fellow-heirs with the Jews in one body under grace
7	3:14-19	Prayer for the body that they may have strength to know
8	3:20, 21	Benediction

It remains, then, to outline the message of the book.

SALUTATION: GREETINGS TO THE BODY, 1:1, 2

I. Doctrinal Message — the body of Christ, 1:3-3:21
  A. Blessings for members of the body, 1:3-14
  B. Prayer that members of the body may have light to know, 1:15-23
  C. Method by which one becomes a member of the body, 2:1-10
  D. Members who belong to the body — both Jew and Gentile, 2:11-3:13
  E. Prayer that members of the body may have strength to know, 3:14-19
  F. Benediction, 3:20, 21

Briefly stated, the message is that the Church, which is the body of Christ, is a new thing. In it both Jews and Gentiles are united to form one organism. Entrance into this body is based on the work of Christ and is by means of faith alone.

This new body is a mystery in that it was not known in previous
ages, and this truth was in a peculiar way committed unto Paul.
Members of the body of Christ are already positionally seated
in the heavenlies, and many other spiritual blessings attend
their daily walk.

By way of illustration of the third type of theological method
of Bible study, two illustrations are provided. In the first, the
Christology of Colossians is developed; in the second the
whole doctrine of temptation is traced throughout the Bible.
We begin the study of Christ as seen in the Book of Colossians
by reading through the book carefully and noting all references
to the person of Christ. These, then, are organized according
to the suggested headings provided in the outline given earlier
in this chapter. In the development of the outline, it will be
necessary to consider items listed under "Trinitarianism," "Soteriology," and "Christology." Here are the theological statements gleaned from Colossians.

1:1 —Christ Jesus
1:2 —peace from our Lord Jesus Christ
1:3 —Father of our Lord Jesus Christ
1:4 —faith in Jesus Christ
1:13—kingdom of the Son of His love
1:14—in whom we have our redemption, the forgiveness of our
       sins
1:15—image of the invisible God, firstborn of all creation
1:16—all things have been created through Him
1:17—He is before all things, and in Him all things hold together
1:18—Head of the body — the church
1:18—Firstborn from the dead
1:19—all fullness in Him
1:20—made peace through the blood of His cross
1:22—accomplished reconciliation
1:24—Church is His body
1:27—Christ in you, the hope of glory
2:3 —treasures of wisdom and knowledge in Him
2:5 —Christ the object of faith
2:6 —walk in Him
2:7 —grow in Him

2:9 —in Him dwelleth the fulness of the Godhead bodily
2:10—Head of principality and power
2:13—He has forgiven us
2:14—fulfilled the law
2:15—judged principalities and powers
3:1 —we are raised with Christ
3:1 —He is seated at the right hand of God
3:4 —Christ is our life
3:4 —Christ shall be manifested and we with Him
3:11—Christ is all, and in all
3:15—the peace of Christ
3:17—do all in His name
3:17—pray in His name
3:24—ye serve the Lord Christ
4:3 —mystery of Christ

The outline constructed from these items will look something like this.

I. His Names
   A. Christ Jesus — 1:1 — signifies mission and humanity
   B. Lord Jesus Christ — 1:3 — signifies lordship, mission, humanity
   C. Lord Christ — 3:24
   D. Son of His love — 1:13
   E. Head of the body — 1:18, 24
II. His Attributes
   A. Personality
      1. Creator — 1:16
      2. Son — 1:13
      3. Resurrection from the dead — 1:18
      4. Forgiver — 2:13
      5. Object of service — 3:24
   B. Omniscience — all treasures of wisdom and knowledge — 2:3
   C. Holiness
      1. Image of invisible God — 1:15
      2. Object of faith — 2:5
      3. He is perfection — 1:29

      D. Love — made peace through the blood of His cross — 1:20

      E. Omnipotence
         1. All created by Him — 1:16
         2. All things hold together by Him — 1:17
         3. All principalities and powers subject to Him — 2:10

      F. Infinity — Christ is all — 3:11

      G. Omnipresence — Christ is in all — 3:11

      H. Eternity — before all things — 1:17; firstborn of all creation — 1:15

III. His Deity
      A. Seen in trinitarian relationship
         1. Son of God — 1:3; 1:13
         2. Image of invisible God — 1:15
         3. Repository of fullness of Godhead — 2:9

      B. Seen in His works
         1. Creator — 1:16
         2. Sustainer — 1:17
         3. Savior — 1:14; 1:20; 1:22; 2:13; 2:14

      C. Seen in other relationships
         1. Head of principalities and powers — 2:10
         2. Object of believer's faith — 1:4; 2:5
         3. Agent in believer's prayer — 3:17
         4. Rule for believer's service — 3:17
         5. Recipient of believer's service — 3:24

IV. His Humanity
      A. Blood spilt — 1:20
      B. Death — 2:15
      C. Resurrection — 2:15; 1:18

 V. His Sufferings and Death
      A. Fulfilled the law — 2:14
      B. Judged principalities and powers — 2:15
      C. Made peace and reconciliation — 1:20, 22
      D. Forgives sins — 2:13

VI. His Resurrection
   A. Firstborn from the dead — 1:18
   B. Guarantee of our resurrection — we are raised with Christ — 3:1
VII. His Session — seated at the right hand of God — 3:1
VIII. His Second Advent — shall be manifested and we with Him — 3:4

Let us turn now to the last example of the theological method: the development of the doctrine of temptation in the Bible. In order to arrive at a complete understanding of the subject, it will be necessary to study the terms "try," "trial," "tempt," "temptation," "test," and related themes by means of a concordance. The findings are so numerous that a complete listing of them is not provided here. After all references relating to this topic have been checked and recorded, seek to discover the meaning of the various words by considering the way they are used or spoken of in their contexts. The final step is to ascertain the main categories into which the subject may be divided and proceed with the finished outline. Since *temptation* is such a vast subject, the writer does not claim to have provided a complete outline of it, but the most significant factors are covered in the following treatment.

I. Individuals Tempt God
   A. Meaning — try
   B. Extent — may tempt all three members of the Godhead
     1. God — Ex. 17:2; Deut. 6:16; Mal. 3:15
     2. Christ — I Cor. 10:9; Matt. 16:1; 19:3
     3. Holy Spirit — Acts 5:9
   C. Results
     1. May stop national blessing — kept many Israelites from the land of promise: Num. 14:23; Ps. 95:11
     2. May cause physical death — Acts 5:9ff; I Cor. 10:9; Ps. 78:31
     3. May result in spiritual leanness — Ps. 106:15
II. God Tempts Individuals
   A. Purpose — to prove, not to lead to sin, cf. Jas. 1:13
   B. Example — Abraham: Gen. 22:1

III. Satan Tempts
    A. Christ — Matt. 4:1ff.; Matt. 1:13; Luke 4:2
        1. Purpose
            a. To lead Him to evil
            b. To prove Him
            c. To enable Him to be a perfect high priest, Heb. 2:18
        2. Areas of temptation
            a. Omnipotence
            b. Will
            c. Other areas — Heb. 4:15
    B. Men
        1. Fact of it — I Cor. 7:5; I Thess. 3:5
        2. Effect of it
            a. To keep sinners or mere professors from salvation — Luke 8:13
            b. To lead to the perfecting of the saints — Jas. 1:3, 4
        3. Victory over Satanic temptation — I Cor. 10:13; II Pet. 2:9
            a. God will not allow us to be tempted above ability to endure
            b. He will provide a way of escape
            c. He provides a reward for those who endure temptation — Jas. 1:1; I Pet. 1:6, 7
            d. He will not allow temptation to separate us from the love of Christ — Rom. 8:35
IV. God Issues Commands Concerning Temptation
    A. The Christian should count it joy to fall into various trials — Jas. 1:2; I Pet. 4:12-14; Rom. 5:3; II Cor. 7:4
    B. Those who are spiritual are to restore those who have succumbed to temptation — Gal. 6:1
    C. Those who are spiritual are to beware lest they too fall into temptation — Gal. 6:1
    D. The believer is commanded to be patient in tribulation — Rom. 12:12
    E. The Christian is exhorted not to tempt fellow Christians to fall — Rom. 14:13; I Cor. 8:9

  F. We are told to beware lest we give Satan an advantage
    to tempt — II Cor. 2:11
 V. God Warns Concerning the Great Tribulation
  A. The whole world is going to come into a time of temp-
    tation or tribulation — Rev. 3:10; Matt. 24:21
  B. This great tribulation will surpass anything the world
    has ever or will ever suffer — Matt. 24:21

SUGGESTIONS FOR FURTHER STUDY

Several suggestions for futher study have already been made
in the text of this chapter, but we pause now to make a few
more. Of particular interest in the development of theological
assumption are those books which do not have a primarily theological message. Ruth, Ecclesiastes, and Lamentations could
well fit into this category; of special note is the Book of Esther,
which does not even once mention the name of God. When one
begins to look for books of the Bible that he may study as a
whole for their theological message, he immediately discovers
that the Old Testament books are usually either narrative or
prophetic in form and that he would do better to consider the
New Testament. Almost any of the Pauline Epistles will serve
his purpose well (with the possible exception of Philemon),
and Hebrews and the Petrine Epistles might be added to the
list. As far as the topical method is concerned, there is almost
no limit to suggestions for further study. One might be interested in themes which relate to salvation: justification, reconciliation, redemption, propitiation, repentance, atonement, faith
and grace; again, he may prefer the study of matters pertaining to his daily Christian walk: confession, abiding, death or
crucifixion or cross, carnality, sanctification, peace, security and
suffering; or possibly he is looking to the future: rewards,
resurrection, eternity, heaven, antichrist, man of sin, millennium,
tribulation and punishment. If the student were to turn to the
theological framework, he could develop many ideas for continued investigation. The doctrine of the Holy Spirit or the
sovereignty of God as seen in Ephesians, the kingship of Christ
as revealed in Matthew, the humanity of Christ as set forth in

Luke, the effects of sin as developed in Romans, the significance of the ascension and present work of Christ, the present activity of Satan, and the organization and practice of the early Church as noted in Acts — these and many more topics will afford great profit and blessing for the student who chooses to develop even to a brief extent what the Scripture has to say about them.

CHAPTER IX

THE LITERARY STUDY OF THE BIBLE

The Bible is great literature, whether it be considered in the Hebrew, Greek, or in translation. To the Hebrews it was a divine national literature; the Old Testament in Greek dress had a profound impact on the Graeco-Roman world, as did the New Testament books when they were produced at a later time. The literature of the Roman Empire after the middle of the second century largely concerned Christian and Biblical themes, and some students of Roman history (when speaking of literary production of the Empire) call the period beginning about 150 the era of Christian literature. In the Middle Ages, when the power of the Church reached a high peak, the copying of the Bible and the discussion of theological issues occupied most of the literary output of the day. With the dawn of the modern era in the sixteenth century, the Bible again took the center of the stage as Hebrew and Greek editions and Latin and several English versions were produced, to say nothing of those in other languages.[1] In recent centuries the Bible has remained a best-seller in several countries, despite stiff competition from secular works; and millions of copies were sold in the first years of publication of the American Standard Version and the Re-

1 Daniel Bomberg produced his Hebrew Bible in 1516-17; Cardinal Ximines printed a New Testament in 1515, but he was not able to market it before Erasmus published his in 1516; the Clementine edition of the Latin Vulgate came out in 1592; Luther's German Bible swept Germany in the 1520's and '30's; Tyndale printed his English New Testament in 1525; Coverdale printed an entire English Bible in 1535; Matthew's Bible, the Great Bible, the Geneva Bible, the Bishop's Bible, the Rheims-Douai Version, and the King James Version — all in English — followed in rapid succession. It is not in any sense intended that this list be considered as complete; it is given merely as an indication of the literary importance of the Bible in the sixteenth century.

vised Standard Version. At the present time even in public schools or colleges and universities, where verbal inspiration is largely a forgotten matter, whole courses are devoted to the study of the Bible as literature. While the Bible is more than great literature, it may be studied profitably from that standpoint; and this work would not be complete without a brief consideration of the literary forms represented in the Bible.[2]

BIBLICAL POETRY

Perhaps the average Sunday-school student who is taught that Job, Psalms, Proverbs, Ecclesiastes, the Song of Solomon, and Lamentations[3] are poetry is quite confused and skeptical because these books do not seen to contain anything like the poetry with which he is acquainted. This is a justifiable reaction since the King James Version quite effectively obscures the literary forms of the Bible. Some of the more recent versions have sought to correct this difficulty by setting the poetic portions in poetic stanza form. Among such versions are Moulton's *The Modern Reader's Bible*, the *American Standard Version*, *The Complete Bible* by Smith and Goodspeed, and the *Revised Standard Version*.[4]

One of the basic principles of Old Testament poetry is parallelism of thought. Probably the most common type of parallelism is *synonymous*, in which the second line essentially repeats the thought of the first. Two verses from the Psalms should suffice to illustrate this form.

---

[2] This chapter differs from the others in this book in that it is mostly devoted to a definition of literary types represented in the Bible, and no particular effort is made to develop examples or suggestions for further study. The writer found that it was quite sufficient to lecture on this subject for one or two class periods and omit assignments of projects to be worked out by the students. The literary study of the Bible works best when an entire semester is given to it. A classic work in the field is Richard G. Moulton's *The Literary Study of the Bible* (Boston: D. C. Heath, 1899), and the present discussion is based in part on that book.

[3] Since almost all poetic representation in the New Testament is quotation from the Old, no effort is made in this chapter to deal with New Testament poetry.

[4] It is not the writer's purpose to discuss the pro and con of liberal or conservative points of view on any of these versions; only the fact that they all arrange Bible poetry in poetic form is called to the attention of the reader here.

Jehovah, how are mine adversaries increased!
Many are they that rise up against me (3:1).

He that sitteth in the heavens will laugh:
The Lord will have them in derision (2:4).

Antithetic parallelism, on the other hand, presents in the second line an idea which is opposite to that of the first line. Psalm 1:6 provides a good example here:

For Jehovah knoweth the way of the righteous;
But the way of the wicked shall perish.

In *synthetic* parallelism, the second or succeeding lines add to or develop the thought of the first line of the verse. This is ably demonstrated in the first two verses of Psalm 1:

Blessed is the man that walketh not in the counsel of the wicked,
Nor standeth in the way of sinners,
Nor sitteth in the seat of scoffers:
But his delight is in the law of Jehovah;
And on his law doth he meditate day and night.

Emblematic parallelism is a type in which the second or succeeding lines give a figurative illustration of the first, as in Psalm 42:1:

As the hart panteth after the water brooks,
So panteth my soul after thee, O God.

Several other types of parallelism could be enumerated here, but they are not very common and it does not seem necessary to include them. Perhaps it should be observed at this point that Hebrew poetry is not limited to couplets but may extend to triplets, quatrains, sextets, and octets. Moreover, parallelism is not restricted to lines but may extend to strophes or stanzas. This may be due in part to the fact that it is characteristic of Hebrew music and speech to chant or recite antiphonally; that is, the leader makes a statement or chants a portion of verse and he is answered by the group he is leading. Sometimes two choirs are involved in the procedure.

A second principle of Hebrew poetry is rhythm; but this does not mean, however, that it is strictly metrical in the sense of adhering to hard-and-fast rules governing balanced numbers of accented and unaccented syllables. Of course it is impossible to display this quality of the original fully in translation. It is possible, though, to observe the figurative nature of Biblical poetry in translation. Numerous rhetorical devices are utilized to great effect. Simile, metaphor, hyperbole, and metonymy are among the many figures of speech that appear. These are discussed and exemplified in the next chapter. Yet one more characteristic of Hebrew poetry should be included here — the alphabetic acrostic. *Acrostic* may be defined as the practice by which sets of letters — as the initial, middle, or final letters of lines or words — when taken in order vertically or horizontally form a word or words. For instance

f orsaking

a ll

i

t ake

h im

may be read in order either vertically or horizontally, and each way a word is formed. In alphabetic acrostic, each letter of the Hebrew alphabet is used to begin a verse, so that read vertically the alphabet is formed; read horizontally, the letter becomes part of the first word of the verse. This principle is beautifully illustrated in the Book of Lamentations, where chapters 1, 2, and 4 are perfect single acrostics — in all three chapters there are twenty-two verses and each begins with a different letter of the Hebrew alphabet in alphabetical order. Chapter 3 has sixty-six verses, a multiple of twenty-two, and three verses begin with each letter of the alphabet. Chapter 5 continues the twenty-two verse pattern, but the arrangement is not acrostic. In Psalm 119 we have another excellent illustration of this arrangement; there eight verses begin with each letter of the Hebrew alphabet. The rather odd-looking words or symbols in the English versions are merely letters or names of letters of the Hebrew alphabet, and each verse in the section under that name begins with the letter listed at the head of the section. Other Psalms are acrostic in nature but are not perfect acrostics.

While the principles of Old Testament poetry have been delineated, it remains to define the types of poetry. Epic is a kind of narrative poetry which deals with heroic action, and it is written in elevated style; drama is acted poetry; and lyric is sung poetry and is reflective in nature. In the Bible there is no verse narrative (epic) as such, but we should hasten to add that Hebrew verse and prose systems overlap. When this is taken into consideration, we realize immediately that epic incidents are scattered through the historical books. Moreover, it must be pointed out that Scripture does contain mixed epic, for example, the story of Balaam (Numbers 22-24).

Probably the best example of Old Testament drama is furnished by the Book of Job; there is found a considerable amount of dramatic dialogue arranged in cycles of development. At the beginning we are allowed to look behind the scenes and discover that all the distress which Job endures is caused by Satanic temptation. Fleeting glimpses of the villain are caught in the early part of the drama. Then the plot thickens as messengers come almost with telegraphic speed to inform him of the misfortune which has befallen him. In short order his wife turns against him, and he is afflicted with physical suffering. The next scene pictures the erstwhile wealthy patriarch sitting by the lonely ash heap at the edge of the city. During the greater part of the drama he engages in a struggle with himself over the question of why he is thus made to suffer; all the while so-called friends offer a variety of suggestions. The tenseness of the situation rises as the reader wonders whether Job will be able to conquer himself. The climax comes as he reasserts his faith in God, and the drama concludes with a pronouncement of divine approval and benediction and restoration of Job's earthly goods.

Lyric is a classification which comprehends many types of poetry. There is the *lyric idyl*, which is a descriptive or narrative poem and is pastoral in nature. The Song of Solomon is classified in this category by those who believe that Solomon disguises himself as a shepherd in order to win the hand of the Shulammite maiden; but those who hold to the interpretation that Solomon endeavors to woo the maiden away from her shepherd lover call it a drama, because a full plot can then be constructed. Another type of lyric is the *ode*, which is difficult to define specifically; but it may be distinguished from other

kinds of lyric by greater elaboration and structural consciousness, and it is characterized by nobility of sentiment and digni-
ty of style. Two very excellent examples of the ode are found
in Deborah's song of Judges 5 and in the song of Miriam and
Moses in Exodus 15. No doubt both of these were recited antiphonally. A third type of lyric is the *elegy*, which is used
primarily in professional mourning. With regard to form, Moulton comments, "In Hebrew the elegaic rhythm is the ordinary
couplet with the second member weakened, by being either
shortened or left destitute of antithesis or parallelism, so much
so that the two are usually printed as a single line with a cae-
sura."[5] Good examples of elegy are found in Lamentations,
Psalms 137, 74, 80, and II Samuel 1:19-27. The literary form
of all of these passages is obscured by the translators. Songs are
also found in the lyric class; these abound in the Psalms, where
they deal with such themes as deliverance, providence, nature,
judgment, trust, and consecration. Likewise, meditations and
prayers appear frequently in Hebrew poetry and are well represented in the Psalms.

BIBLICAL PROSE

Biblical prose divides into three classifications: history — the
branch of knowledge which records and explains past events;
rhetoric — prose for presentation; and philosophy — organized
reflection. Moulton describes five kinds of Biblical history.[6]
Primal or primitive history covers the period preceding the
appearance of the Hebrews as a nation. Constitutional history
appears in Exodus, Leviticus, and Numbers; such a name is
assigned because these books provide a record of the revelation
of the government of God and the events pertaining thereto.
Incidental history is so named because certain books of the
Bible consist mainly of epic incidents joined together by sum-
maries and a variety of other connectives; Joshua, Judges, I
Samuel, and possibly Ruth may be classified here. Ruth is sometimes considered to be an epic idyl because of its pastoral
nature; others would call it a short story. Regular history, a

5 Moulton, *op. cit.*, p. 168.
6 *Ibid.*, pp. 251-259.

systematic account of successive reigns with incidents narrated historically, is found in such books as II Samuel, I Kings, II Kings, much of Chronicles, and Esther. The fifth classification is ecclesiastical history. Old Testament books such as parts of Chronicles, Ezra, and Nehemiah, which deal with Jewish religion and the restoration of Jewish religion after the exile; and New Testament books such as the Gospels and Acts, which narrate the founding of Christianity, are placed in this category.

Rhetoric, a second major branch of prose, is the art of expressive discourse or literary composition. It embodies both spoken and written rhetoric. The former is best illustrated in the book of Deuteronomy, which is a record of condensed speeches delivered by Moses to the children of Israel. Other shorter portions, such as the propaganda speeches of Rabshekah in II Kings and II Chronicles, could well be included here. Written rhetoric comprehends the whole epistolary field of the New Testment. Epistles of pastoral intercourse or pure epistles are those which have the full form of epistolary correspondence, beginning with a salutation from the apostle, continuing with a greeting to a particular church or fellow worker, and ending with further salutations and greetings and sometimes with an autograph message. Books included in this classification are I and II Corinthians, Galatians, Philippians, I and II Thessalonians, I and II Timothy, Titus, Philemon, II and III John (Moulton prefers to class James and I John with the wisdom literature). Hebrews and Romans may be designated as epistolary treatises. The former is a doctrinal treatise and lacks epistolary form; while the latter, though possessing personal contact, is a doctrinal letter addressed to a church which the Apostle has never visited. The third type of epistle is that which Moulton has chosen to call epistolary manifesto.[7] Included in this group are Colossians, Ephesians, I and II Peter, and Jude. Colossians has epistolary form but is called forth by incipient Gnosticism; Ephesians seems to be encyclical in form (*at Ephesus* does not appear in the best manuscripts); I Peter is necessitated by persecution and its consequent suffer-

---

[7] *Ibid.,* p. 266.

ing; and II Peter and Jude are manifestos called forth by evil which is attacking the church from within.

One more type of literature remains to be discussed[8] — the philosophy or wisdom literature of the Bible. Biblical philosophy concerns itself with the riddle of life and is related constantly to the nature of one's conduct in life; that is to say, it is essentially an ethical philosophy. Sometimes the reflection on life is an extremely brief epigrammatic saying and is embodied in a single proverbial couplet; at other times it may be longer and could then be classified as an essay on some aspect of life — both of these are found in the Book of Proverbs. In Ecclesiastes, philosophical reflection is applied to life as a whole, and particular observations are made on the general problem of the meaning of existence.

It is sincerely hoped that the consideration of the Bible from the literary standpoint will open new vistas of appreciation to the reverent student of the Word of God. He already puts a high premium on its message; let him go on to develop an aesthetic evaluation of the vehicle in which that message is couched. Let him come to the realization that the Christian need not feel that his Bible is an antiquated museum piece despised by the scholarship of the day, but rather may he take pride in the fact that it is a high quality literary production that can hold its own in the highest circles of culture and refinement.

[8] Perhaps the reader has been wondering about Biblical prophecy as a literary form. Prophetic literature embodies many types of literature. Prophetic discourse may often be classed as spoken rhetoric; it may also assume the form of history—written in advance; or there may be description of symbolical actions as is true in the case of Jeremiah; again, the prophet may lapse into poetic form in the delivery of his message. Then there is the prophetic burden or doom which is often pronounced on individuals or nations for their sin.

CHAPTER X

THE RHETORICAL METHOD

Rhetoric is the art of expressive discourse or literary composition. Its artistic development is achieved in large measure by means of frequent utilization of figures of speech. As indicated in the last chapter, figurative language is an element which contributes to making Hebrew poetry "poetic," and it is a term descriptive of a whole field of Biblical prose; as such, the rhetorical method of Bible study is in a sense merely a division of the literary method. It is felt that there are sufficient distinguishing characteristics and differences of purpose of this method, however, to justify a separate chapter. In the first place, the rhetorical method is not merely a literary study; it is a consideration of the art of expressing truth. Divine truth is often abstract and difficult for finite minds to understand. There must be, then, just as great an effort on the part of God to accommodate doctrine to the human mind as there is to relate the person of God to human thinking. The latter is accomplished by assigning to God such members as eyes, arms and hands; the former is executed by means of figures of speech, in which the unknown is stated in terms familiar to the man on the street. Of course, figurative speech is also useful in emphasizing Biblical truth. Second, while a study of the literary form of a book of the Bible is a whole field of its own, the recognition of figures of speech can be carried on as a small part of other methods of Bible study. Third, careful attention to the figurative language of the Bible will improve the oral and written effectiveness of the Christian worker because he will in that way unconsciously develop his style of expression. In this present study the figures of speech are defined and illustrated, and a few suggestions for further study are made. It seems unnecessary to develop an entire book according to the rhetorical method.

Figures of Speech

Simile. Simile is the direct comparison of two things essentially different, on the basis of similarity in one or more respects. The similarity is usually noted by *like, as,* or *so.* To say "John's literary style is like Jane's" is not simile because two like things are being compared. A better illustration is found in the statement that "The airplane is like a bird in its flight" or in a quotation from Bacon, "Virtue is like a rich stone, best plain set." Scripture abounds in the use of simile; a few verses will suffice here.

> He hath made me to dwell in dark places, as those that have been long dead (Ps. 143:3c).
>
> and the rich, in that he is made low: because as the flower of the grass he shall pass away. For the sun ariseth with the scorching wind, and withereth the grass; and the flower thereof falleth, and the grace of the fashion of it perisheth; so also shall the rich man fade away in his goings (Jas. 1:10, 11).
>
> Come now, and let us reason together, saith Jehovah: though your sins be as scarlet, they shall be as white as snow; though they be red like crimson, they shall be as wool (Is. 1:18).

Metaphor. Metaphor is indirect comparison of two things by establishment of identity between them, a figure in which one thing is made identical with another, or in which the two are spoken of as though they were identical even when one cannot perform all the functions of the other. Generally the writer asserts that one thing is another — there is the substitution of the name of one thing for the name of the other. In it likeness is implied rather than stated explicitly. For instance, Shelley, after he had once escaped death by drowning, wrote, "Death is the veil which those who live call life; they sleep, and it is lifted." Here death is called a veil but it is only like a veil; in the implied comparison the name of the one (death) is substituted for the other (veil). A similar usage is seen in the fol-

lowing two quotations, the first by Herbert Read and the second
by Marullus in Shakespeare's *Julius Caesar*.

> But meaning is an arrow that reaches its mark when least encum-
> bered with feathers.

> You blocks, you stones, you worse than senseless things!

In the latter quotation, the cruel men of Rome are likened to
stones — inanimate objects, without a heart. It should be observed that if the statement had read "You are like stones,"
the figure would have been a simile because the comparison is
no longer implied and a specific word of comparison is used.
An excellent Biblical example of metaphor is found in Galatians 2:9: ". . . James and Cephas and John, they who were
reputed to be pillars . . ." Note also in this connection Proverbs
23:27: "For a harlot is a deep ditch; and a foreign woman is a
narrow pit." In the Galatians reference, the Apostles are like-
ened to pillars in that they are main supports of the Church;
while in the Proverbs passage a harlot is compared to a deep
ditch because she is a pitfall to men.

Allegory. Allegory is metaphor extended to form a story,
real or fictitious, in which a series of actions is symbolic of
other actions; and the details of the story are made to convey
a meaning different from the literal meaning of the events set
forth. Familiar allegories are Bunyan's *Pilgrim's Progress* and
C. S. Lewis' *The Screwtape Letters*. Allegory is used very spar-
ingly in Scripture because the Bible deals in fact and presents
a message which is, for the most part, subject to literal interpretation and therefore capable of being understood by individuals who have not advanced too far academically or are
young in years. A good example of allegory is found in the
Book of Galatians; but even here it is not to be taken that the
account of Abraham's two children is not true. Rather, Paul by
means of allegorical application is merely bringing out a point
that is latent in the Genesis passage anyway; and he is not
guilty of finding in the Genesis story some mystical message that
violates historical reality.

> Tell me, ye that desire to be under the law, do ye not hear the
> law? For it is written, that Abraham had two sons, one by the hand-

maid, and one by the freewoman. Howbeit the son by the handmaid is born after the flesh; but the son by the freewoman is born
through promise. Which things contain an allegory: for these
women are two covenants; one from mount Sinai, bearing children
unto bondage, which is Hagar. Now this Hagar is mount Sinai in
Arabia and answereth to the Jerusalem that now is: for she is in
bondage with her children. But the Jerusalem that is above is free,
which is our mother. For it is written,

> Rejoice, thou barren that bearest not;
> Break forth and cry, thou that travailest not:
> For more are the children of the desolate than of her
>   that hath the husband.

Now we, brethren, as Isaac was, are children of promise. But as then
he that was born after the flesh persecuted him that was born after
the Spirit, so also it is now. Howbeit what saith the scripture? Cast
out the handmaid and her son: for the son of the handmaid shall
not inherit with the son of the freewoman. Wherefore, brethren,
we are not children of a handmaid, but of the freewoman (Gal.
4:21-31).

Analogy. An analogy is usually a rather full comparison,
showing or implying several points of similarity between unlike
things. It differs from allegory in that it does not try to tell
a story. One of the best Scriptural examples of analogy is
found in John 15:1-9.

I am the true vine, and my Father is the husbandman. Every
branch in me that beareth not fruit, he taketh it away: and every
branch that beareth fruit, he cleanseth it, that it may bear more
fruit. Already ye are clean because of the word which I have spoken
unto you. Abide in me, and I in you. As the branch cannot bear
fruit of itself, except it abide in the vine; so neither can ye, except
ye abide in me. I am the vine, ye are the branches: He that abideth
in me, and I in him, the same beareth much fruit: for apart from
me ye can do nothing. If a man abide not in me, he is cast forth
as a branch, and is withered; and they gather them, and cast them
into the fire, and they are burned. If ye abide in me, and my
words abide in you, ask whatsoever ye will, and it shall be done
unto you. Herein is my Father glorified, that ye bear much fruit;
and so shall ye by my disciples. Even as the Father hath loved me,
I also have loved you: abide in my love.

Irony. In the use of irony one implies something markedly
different, sometimes even the opposite, from what is actually

said, in order to achieve humor or sarcasm. In Galatians 4:18, Paul uses this figure when he says, "But it is good to be zealously sought in a good manner at all times, and not only when I am present with you." The actual historical situation was that the Galatian believers had turned against him unto another gospel — that of legalism.

Personification. This is the attribution of life or human qualities to inanimate objects or abstractions. Thomas Sackville uses this figure of speech in his description of age:

> Crookbacked he was, tooth-shaken, and blear-eyed,
> Went on three feet, and sometime crept on four,
> With old lame bones that rattled by his side. . . .
> His withered fist still knocking at Death's door.

Following are a few Biblical examples of personification.

> Then the lust, when it hath conceived, beareth sin: and the sin, when it is fullgrown, bringeth forth death (Jas. 1:15).
>
> And he prayed again; and the heaven gave rain, and the earth brought forth her fruit (Jas. 5:18).
>
> Wisdom hath builded her house; she hath hewn out her seven pillars: she hath killed her beasts; she hath mingled her wine; she hath also furnished her table: she hath sent forth her maidens; she crieth upon the highest places of the city (Prov. 9:1-3).

Apostrophe. Closely related to personification is apostrophe. It may be defined as the feigned turning from one's audience to address directly a person, or, more frequently, a thing, an abstract idea, or imaginary object as if it were a person. Examples of this figure of speech are seen in Hosea 13:14 and I Corinthians 15:55:

> O death, where are thy plagues? O Sheol, where is thy destruction?
>
> O death, where is thy victory? O death, where is thy sting?

Hyperbole. This figure employs fanciful exaggeration; it does not intend to deceive but rather to emphasize a statement or situation in order to intensify its impression. Hyperbole is often used in slang expressions such as "I'm all ears" or "I'm thrilled to pieces." By way of further illustration, King Lear, in his frenzy, says:

> Had I your tongue and eyes, I'd use them so
> That heaven's vault should crack.

Paul also utilizes hyperbole in his epistles:

> If I speak with the tongues of men and of angels . . . (I Cor. 13:1a).

> . . . for I bear you witness, that, if possible, ye would have plucked out your eyes and given them to me (Gal. 4:15).

Rhetorical question. In the use of rhetorical question, a writer or speaker poses a question to which he does not expect an answer; the device is used to attract the attention of the reader or hearer. This is such a commonly used figure that it needs no elaboration here. One example should suffice: "Is Christ divided? was Paul crucified for you? or were ye baptized into the name of Paul?" (I Cor. 1:13).

Antithesis. Antithesis may be defined as the strong contrast of ideas, often through parallel construction. One of the most familiar examples of this figure of speech is Psalm 1:6: "For Jehovah knoweth the way of the righteous; but the way of the wicked shall perish."

Litotes. Litotes is an understatement, the opposite of hyperbole and often a form of irony, the stating of an idea in negative terms, the affirmation of a fact by denying its opposite. One would be using litotes if he said "Dempsey was not a bad fighter" or "Socrates was not a bad teacher." Beowulf used this figure when he said, "I . . . swore not many oaths wrongfully"; he meant that he was guileless in swearing and that he never broke a pledge. Paul utilized litotes, too, when he stated in Galatians 5:10: "I have confidence to youward in the Lord, that ye will be none otherwise minded. . . ."

Metonymy. Metonymy is the substitution of one term for another closely associated with it or suggested by it, such as a *dish* for something to eat and *capital* and *labor* for employers and workmen. *Circumcision* is often used in the New Testament in place of *Jew*, e.g., "if so be that God is one, and he shall justify the circumcision by faith . . ." (Rom. 3:30). In this same verse *uncircumcision* is substituted for *Gentile*. Paul uses *seed* to stand for *Christ* in Galatians 3:19.

Synecdoche. Synecdoche, very closely related to metonymy, is a figure in which the name of a part of something is given when the whole is meant (*"mouths* to feed," *"sail* in the offing," "plant employing sixty *hands"*) or the name of the whole when a part is meant (someone says that *"Minnesota* won" when the team from Minnesota is what really won; *"England* meets *America* in the Davis Cup matches," when it is teams from the respective countries which meet). When James says to the twelve tribes of the dispersion, "Cleanse your hands, ye sinners; and purify your hearts, ye doubleminded" (Jas. 4:8b), he is obviously using *hands* and *hearts* to stand for the whole person. The same figure is used in Galatians 1:16b, where Paul writes, "I conferred not with flesh and blood."

The writer recognizes that other figures of speech do exist; but some of these, while valuable to a speech student, do not appear frequently in Scripture. Moreover, it was felt that some rhetorical forms are, in usage and meaning, so nearly like those included here that it was unnecessary to discuss them.

SUGGESTIONS FOR FURTHER STUDY

Obviously, some of these figures of speech can be found in every book of the Bible, and one might make the identification of rhetorical form an incidental part of the study of any book; but certain books of the Bible abound in figurative phraseology and will therefore provide an opportunity for applying this method to a whole book. Since figurative language is a characteristic of Hebrew poetry, any of the poetic works of the Old Testament — Job, Psalms, Proverbs, Ecclesiastes, Song of Solomon, and Lamentations — may be profitably studied in this way. Many passages in the Prophets are replete with figurative language because those men of God sought to make their language forceful as they hurled accusations against their evil countrymen and godless nations around them. The discourse sections of the Gospels will also repay the student's rhetorical investigation as Jesus was the Master Teacher and used much illustration and figurative language in getting his point across. Paul, too, was an able teacher and lecturer; and most of his epistles utilize figures of speech in abundance, but those in which he is dealing with some special error — Galatians, Corinthians, etc. — seem to call forth a greater rhetorical effort on his part. Last, let it be noted that the Book of James, which has a Jewish or oriental flavor greater than that of most of the other New Testament books, uses a large number of rhetorical devices.

CHAPTER XI

THE GEOGRAPHICAL METHOD

Geography comes from two Greek words which mean *the description of the earth;* but since the basic definition of this term is so close to that of geology, it is necessary to be more explicit in demonstrating the scope of the science. Let us say, then, that geography is the systematized knowledge regarding the earth's surface, its physical features and phenomena, the living creatures upon it, especially man, and the political divisions of mankind. Scientists speak of mathematical geography, which deals with dimensions, figure, and movements of the earth; physical geography, the configuration of the earth's crust; biological geography, the distribution of living organisms on the surface of the globe; and human geography, the distribution of mankind in relation to the conditions of geographical environment. It will readily be seen that geography is a composite science, making use of astronomy, applied mathematics, physics, geology, and anthropology. Since mathematical geography deals with matters almost entirely apart from Scripture and biological geography treats of material which will be discussed in the chapter on the scientific method of Bible study, these two fields of geographical study are largely omitted from the present consideration. In an effort to be practical, non-technical terminology is adopted in this chapter.

Our brief consideration of the field of geography includes (1) the land — its location, size, elevation, natural resources, rainfall, quality of soil, and political and natural barriers; (2) cities and their location; (3) bodies of water — lakes, rivers, and seas; (4) the location of people on the land and the effect of geography on the people.

The geographical method of Bible study may be developed in relation to an entire book or portion of it, in consideration of a country mentioned in the Bible, as background for the life of a Biblical personality, or as a contextual study of a Biblical narrative. In working out any of these approaches, it should be helpful to make notations on as many of the following items as a given text will allow.

1. Countries — their boundaries and location.

2. Configuration of territory under consideration — rivers, mountains, lakes, general elevation, and observations on their importance to the narrative at hand. Are bodies of water and mountains named in other passages of the Bible?

3. Cities — where located and at what elevation? Are they mentioned elsewhere in Scripture? If so, in what connection?

4. Why is it significant that this event occurred in this geographical context and not in some other?

5. What can be told about the geographical area by the kind of animals and plants to be found there?

6. Are any of the geographical terms seemingly symbolic? For example, in the Prophets mountains sometimes stand for the rulers or authority.

7. What are the effects of geography on history or the Biblical narrative or the people of an area in matters of basic economy or livelihood, food and dress, outlook on life, transportation, building materials, writing materials, national and international relations, and the frequency of wars.

DEVELOPMENT OF METHOD

A consideration of the geographical context of the events leading up to the birth of Moses and of the first forty years of his life has been chosen in order to provide an example of the geographical method of Bible study. Our investigation is limited to Exodus 1:1 - 2:15a. The first step is to tabulate all matters, in the passage under consideration, that relate in any way to geographical research. This list includes the following: Egypt, store cities — Pithom and Raamses, service in mortar and in brick, and in all manner of service in the field, river, bulrushes, slime, pitch, flags by the river, and sand. It now remains to develop these geographical items in relation to the outline detailed above.

1. Egypt is located in the northeast corner of the continent of Africa. The Mediterranean Sea on the north, the Libyan desert on the west, Nubia (Sudan) on the south, and the Red Sea and the Sinai Peninsula on the east serve as boundaries.

2. The configuration of the land is intimated by three terms found in the text — *river, sand* and *field.* The river is the Nile; sand tells of the great desert wastes; and the mention of fields indicates that there is a substantial amount of arable farm land — not all is desert. Someone has said, "Egypt is the Nile," and such a statement is not hard to substantiate. Were it not for the Nile, which brings water from the Ethiopian high-lands, this area of North Africa would be nothing but desert waste. Until 1902, when the Aswan dam was completed, the Nile overflowed its banks annually, laying a deposit of rich soil and watering the thirsty land. During the rest of the year the river furnished water for irrigation, domesticated animals and personal needs. Moreover, silt piled up at the mouth of the Nile to form the famous delta of Egypt. Some of the best farm land was to be found here; and it was in the Eastern section of the delta, in an area known as Goshen, that the Is-raelites were permitted to settle. Along the Nile south of the delta stretched a ribbon of verdant territory varying in width from about nine to thirty miles; the rest of Egypt was desert (except for a few oases), receiving less than one inch of rain-fall per year. Although they are not mentioned in Exodus, there were mountains in Egypt. Located mainly along the Red Sea coast, they frequently reached a height of 6,000 feet.

3. Two cities are mentioned in the Exodus passage — Pithom and Raamses; these are located in the delta, where the children of Israel were living at the time. Though there has been quite a controversy over the identification of these towns, it seems best on the basis of present evidence to equate Pithom with Tell Retabeh and Raamses with Tanis, a Hyksos capital. The main cities of Egypt — Memphis and Thebes — are located to

the south of the delta and do not figure in the Biblical narrative at this point, but they are mentioned elsewhere in Scripture.

4. It is significant that these events occurred in this geographical context because (1) the providence of God is represented in the fact that the Israelites were permitted to come to Egypt at government expense and live on some of the best land in the nation in the midst of plenty, while much of the rest of the Near East was starving. (2) The Egyptians would have had less control over the Hebrews if they had been in Palestine or somewhere else at this time. (3) Some of the bovine worship of Egypt rubbed off on the Jews, as is demonstrated in the erection by Aaron of the calf in the wilderness. (4) God could get greater glory from a demonstration of His power on a strong nation than He could in dealing with one of the weak peoples of the Near East of that day. (5) Moses was permitted to get a very superior education, which helped to qualify him for his task as leader of his people (Acts 7:22) and as author of the Pentateuch. (6) The type of burdens placed on the Hebrews was very different from what it would have been if they were in bondage somewhere else. Building with mud brick was not so common in Palestine, where rainfall averaged something like twenty-five inches per year. Moreover, the Hebrew men must have been extremely miserable if their work included the cutting of irrigation canals, for they would then have been exposed to the hot Egyptian sun as they labored in the trenches where no breezes could reach them; undoubtedly they stood in water much of the time. At certain times of the year the humidity and heat of the delta area are almost unbearable when one is not working, to say nothing of the agony endured if one is forced to engage in hard labor.

5. Bulrushes and flags are the only Egyptian plants mentioned in the text under consideration, and they do tell a little bit about the geography of the area. "Bulrushes" is the translation of a Hebrew word which may be identified with papyrus — a reed which grows in marshy areas, frequently to a height of ten to fifteen feet. It was often used for the con-

struction of lighter river vessels, as the ark which was made for Moses (slime and pitch of Exodus 2:3 were asphalt and bitumen, probably imported from the Dead Sea region). "Flags" were another of the Egyptian reeds which grew in marshy spots along the Nile.

6. Since none of the terms in the passage under study seem to be symbolic, we come now to the last question suggested in the plan for developing the geographical method — the effect of geography on the narrative or the people of the area. The progress of the historical narrative is affected by the fact that the Hebrews were located in some of the best farm and grazing land of Egypt; and since arable land was at a premium, the Egyptians were probably worried about the fact that such a large percentage of it was passing into the hands of foreigners. Further, the increasing foreign element posed a threat to the national government and perpetuation of native traditions. It must be said, too, that geography determined the kind of hardships to which the Hebrews were subjected. The natural resources of the area were not great, and the Nile permitted profitable farming; so the people were largely restricted to agrarian occupations. Furthermore, the slight amount of rainfall permitted the use of sun-dried brick as a building material; abundant quantities of strongly adhesive clay were to be found along the banks of the Nile, as well as in other places throughout Egypt. While stone was used for temples, palaces, and public buildings; city walls, forts, temple enclosures, and lesser buildings were made from mud brick. The geography further affected the people of the area in the type of material the Egyptians used for writing (limitless supplies of papyrus were available along the Nile); the type of clothing they wore (cotton and flax were products of the soil); and the political unity of the land — the river tended to unify the whole Nile Valley, and natural barriers north of the first cataract were few.

SUGGESTIONS FOR FURTHER STUDY

Numerous approaches may be taken to the geographical method of Bible study. Whole books of the Bible or portions of books might be selected as units to be considered in this way. Ruth, Jonah, or Joshua provide interesting book studies; while portions of books that contain rather extensive geographical references are Isaiah 13 - 23, Jeremiah 46 - 51, and Ezekiel 25 - 32, 35, 38, 39. The latter references all relate to nations against which the Prophets pronounce warning or doom.

Second, the geography of many countries mentioned in the Bible could be developed. Included in the list will be such great nations as Persia, Babylon, Rome, Greece, Assyria, Egypt, and lesser powers such as Moab and Edom.

Third, Biblical biography yields much profitable information when studied from this standpoint. The life stories of Jesus, Abraham, Isaac, Jacob, Elijah, Elisha, Samson, Ahab, and Jehu take on new significance when their geographical setting is fully investigated.

Fourth, many Scriptural narratives are better understood and more vividly visualized when seen against their geographical backdrop. We might place in this category the wilderness wanderings of the children of Israel, the account of any of Paul's three missionary journeys or the voyage to Rome, the Hebrew conquest of Palestine, the military march of Abraham in Genesis 14, the wanderings of David while fleeing from Saul, the conquests of David after he became king, and the military ventures of Deborah and Barak.

A host of special studies might also be attempted. The student would certainly enjoy a development of the geographical features of the glories of the reign of Solomon as reflected in I Kings 9:10-28. Blessing would be derived from a serious investigation of the significance of such great mountains of the Bible as Nebo, Sinai, Ararat, Hor, Gilboa, Moriah, and the Mount of Olives. Great rivers of the Bible and their relation to the Biblical narrative should also prove to be a topic worthy of consideration; the Nile, Tigris, Euphrates, Jordan, the Abana, and Pharpar are among those that would appear on this list.

BIBLIOGRAPHY

In addition to such basic reference works as the *Encyclopaedia Britannica, Americana Encyclopedia, Encyclopedia of the Social Sciences, The New Schaff-Herzog Encyclopedia of Religious Knowledge,* the *International Standard Bible Encyclopedia, Webster's Geographical Dictionary,* and Hastings' *Dictionary of the Bible,* the following books will prove to be helpful in developing the geographical method of Bible study.

Adams, J. M., *Biblical Backgrounds* (Nashville: Broadman Press, 1938).

Barton, George A., *Archaeology and the Bible* (7th ed.; Philadelphia: American Sunday-School Union, 1937).

Dalman, Gustaf, *Sacred Sites and Ways,* translated by Paul P. Levertoff (London: Society for Promoting Christian Knowledge, 1935).

Finegan, Jack, *Light from the Ancient Past* (Princeton: Princeton University Press, 1946).

Free, Joseph P., *Archaeology and Bible History* (Wheaton, Illinois: Van Kampen Press, 1950).

Hurlbut, Jesse Lyman, *A Bible Atlas,* (New York: Rand McNally & Company, 1910).

Miller, Madeleine S., and J. Lane, *Encyclopedia of Bible Life* (New York: Harper & Brothers, 1944).

————, *Harper's Bible Dictionary* (New York: Harper & Brothers, 1952).

Ramsay, W. M., *The Cities of St. Paul* (London: Hodder & Stoughton, 1907, reprinted by Baker Book House).

————, *St. Paul the Traveller and the Roman Citizen* (8th ed.; London: Hodder & Stoughton, 1905, reprinted by Baker Book House).

Smith, William, *Smith's Bible Dictionary* (rev. ed.; Grand Rapids: Zondervan Publishing House, 1953).

Wright, George E., and Floyd V. Filson, *The Westminster Historical Atlas to the Bible* (Philadelphia: The Westminster Press, 1946).

CHAPTER XII

THE SOCIOLOGICAL METHOD

Sociology is the scientific study of society, and as such it deals with group behavior and human relationships of all kinds. The science of sociology is, therefore, as vast and as intricate as society itself. It is possible, however, to organize the whole field of general sociology in a limited number of categories, omitting special studies like social psychology, schools of sociological thought, and the history of social thought.

Basic to all social institutions and relationships is the family, the study of which may be considered under the headings of biological necessity, the effects of the small and large family system on society, status of women, and the functions of the family. The latter are four in number: (1) social control of sex expression and reproduction; (2) care and socialization of children — heredity and environment must be noted here; (3) economic cooperation; (4) companionship and affection.

Logically we should turn next to community organization and relationships, for the community is merely the combination of a number of families. In this field, discussion relates to the association between the individual and the community; the care of the community exercised on behalf of poor, sick, disabled, or criminals; and the types of community organization. Communities may be classified politically — organized or unorganized, state or national, international, and intranational; economically — agricultural, commercial, and industrial; religiously — individuals living in groups for religious reasons, e.g., convents; geographically — regional, urban, and suburban; and educationally — colleges or academies organize their campuses virtually as towns and carry on many of the normal functions of a town.

A third category of sociological investigation comprehends the whole range of government as a social institution. Subjects to be considered here are the relation of government and its subjects, an investigation of the judicial activity of government, and a definition of the types of government, which are three — unitary, federal, and confederate. In the unitary type, officers of the central government have complete legal control of the local officers; in the state, on the other hand, local units have a certain amount of autonomy and are protected from too much control on the part of national officials, and a representative form of government is maintained; a confederation is the opposite of a unitary organization — the local units have control of the central government, which is a loose sort of arrangement.

Communication and distribution constitute another division of sociological inquiry. Types and speed of travel, the distribution or maldistribution of goods and its effect on society, the speed and nature of communication, and the control of news or propaganda methods are all included in this classification. Perhaps it would be of value to list at this point some of the basic propaganda devices: (1) name calling — do not bother to prove your point about an enemy; just label him in such a way that many will turn against him; (2) glittering generalities — vague terminology and high-sounding language to secure acceptance of your ideas; (3) prestige — the use of testimonials by important persons to sell a product or get across a point; (4) card stacking — slight or gross misrepresentation of fact in order to rally support for one's position; (5) the band wagon technique — appeals to people to do the popular thing.

A fifth classification of sociological study relates to goods — their consumption and the distribution of income which permits their purchase; property — whether it is privately or state-owned and how much protection is given by the state to real and personal property; production — the human services, natural resources, and capital goods involved in it; and free private enterprise — the role of profit and competition and governmental control or restrictions on enterprise.

Sociology also concerns itself with labor and management

relations. Involved here are the questions of why workers are hired and fired, the kinds of work employees are called upon to do, sources of friction between employers and employees, and methods of solving these problems.

A seventh category of sociological research deals with race and racialism. Not only are the areas of conflict between the major races discussed, but nationality clashes must also be included in this investigation.

The last sociological classification involves social relations promoting richer living — religion, education, recreation, and the arts. The profit of religion to the individual and society and the conflicts which it engenders; the value of education as an adjustment, to enable one to contribute to society, and to help him to earn his way in society; recreation and the arts as they contribute to the development of wholesome personality and provide employment for many — all these have a vital part to play in a complete study of sociology.

It should not be necessary to discuss at length the means of applying this sociological material to Scripture. Since human nature has been essentially the same ever since the fall of Adam, Biblical personalities and social groups faced many of the same conflicts and issues that confront modern society; the main difference is that technological advance has heightened a number of these areas of contention and changed some of the methods used in solving them. This being true, the student should find it possible to evaluate sociological issues of Old and New Testament times from the standpoint of his own context; and between his experience and the utilization of the brief outline of the subject suggested in this chapter, he should be able to organize a sociological analysis of given portions of the Bible. In an effort to make the prosecution of this method a little clearer, an example is provided in a sociological interpretation of the Book of Ruth, and the student is furnished with a listing of study projects for his future use. Perhaps a careful reading of these suggestions will help to demonstrate the extensive use to which this method may be put in Bible study.

DEVELOPMENT OF EXAMPLE

In the general secular interpretation of the social sciences, the approach is horizontal; that is, relationships are considered on one plane only — the human. A Christian interpretation, on the other hand, must be viewed as perpendicular or pyramidal; not only must the relationships between individuals or groups and their environment be evaluated correctly, but God must be brought into the account. Certainly such is the case in a sociological interpretation of the Book of Ruth. Naomi viewed her family condition at the opening of the story as being due to the interference of God. She said that the hand of the Lord had been against her (1:13, 20-21), with the result that her husband and two sons had died; and so she encouraged her daughters-in-law to return to their homes in Moab where the Lord would care for them (1:8). This reference to the activity of God among men is seen throughout the book, even in the latter part of chapter four where it is recognized that Ruth's child, Obed, was a gift from God.

As we come to study further the subject of the family in Ruth, we realize that procreation was of primary concern to the Israelite; there was a very special desire that one should have children to perpetuate his name and occupy his inheritance (4:5, 10, 11). To insure this perpetuation of one's line an ingenious provision had been made in the Law; this was called levirate marriage, from the Latin *levir* which means *brother-in-law*. Deuteronomy 25:5-10 embodies the divine arrangement:

> If brethren dwell together, and one of them die, and have no son, the wife of the dead shall not be married without unto a stranger: her husband's brother shall go in unto her, and take her to him to wife, and perform the duty of a husband's brother unto her. And it shall be, that the first-born that she beareth shall succeed in the name of his brother that is dead, that his name be not blotted out of Israel. And if the man like not to take his brother's wife, then his brother's wife shall go up to the gate unto the elders, and say, My husband's brother refuseth to raise up unto his brother a name in Israel; he will not perform the duty of a husband's brother unto me. Then the elders of his city shall call him, and speak unto him: and if he stand, and say, I like not to take her; then shall his brother's wife come unto him in the presence of the

elders, and loose his shoe from off his foot, and spit in his face; and she shall answer and say, So shall it be done unto the man that doth not build up his brother's house. And his name shall be called in Israel, The house of him that hath his shoe loosed.

When a brother-in-law already had family responsibilities, the next of kin would be eligible to fulfill the marriage obligation. Obviously, the *rest* spoken of in Ruth 1:9 and 3:1 refers to this redemption on the part of the near relative — a kinsman redeemer, which act carries with it not only legal protection of one's property but the responsibility of family perpetuation. The matter of the kinsman redeemer appears in Ruth 2:20; 3:3, 9, 12, 13; and 4:1-10.

Closely related to this question is that of the stature of women in Hebrew society. That they were respected and treated quite well is obvious from the whole tenor of the book. Widows retained possession of property which had belonged to their deceased husbands (4:3); but apparently the legal right to such property was not considered permanent, since they were expected to seek the office of a kinsman redeemer, and property would then be placed in the name of the male member of the household. There is no evidence in the book that women were in any way abused or treated in an unkindly fashion. Several references show that they worked alongside the men in the field — 2:3, 8, 9, 21, 23. From the picture presented in chapter three, it would seem that they had something to say about the choice of a husband.

In turning to a discussion of community organization and relationships, we discover that the stage for the drama of Ruth is set in and around Bethlehem. That the town was small is to be gathered from Ruth 1:19, where the statement is made that all the city gathered around Naomi and Ruth when they returned; that it was an agricultural community is gathered from the statement about the barley harvest in 1:22, and the harvest scenes elsewhere in the book. Since the account of the birth of Christ mentions shepherds watching flocks in the area, we may take it that this was an agricultural and sheep-herding community. Apparently business and legal transactions were carried on at the gate of the city (Ruth 4:1ff.), just as they were at Sodom in the days of Lot (Gen. 19:1). The effect of famine on community life is clear from Ruth 1:1, where such a catastrophe seemingly made it necessary for Naomi and her family to leave Bethlehem ten years earlier. Provision for the poor of the community was made by leaving some grain in the field at the time of harvest (Lev. 23:22); Ruth (2:2) takes advantage of this means of procuring food for herself and her mother-in-law.

The third category of sociological investigation concerns itself with government as a social institution. Not much can be gleaned from Ruth on this subject, but Ruth 1:1 mentions the fact that the narrative takes place during the days of the Judges. Since every judge probably did not rule over all of Palestine, and since there were periods of apostasy between their terms, government of this period could be variously defined. In an area where the judges were particularly powerful, government would be more unitary in nature; in periods between judges, when "every man did that which was right in his own eyes," the condition was anarchy; the general situation, however, may be labeled as confederacy because the Israelite tribes were a loosely knit society during this period.

Our consideration turns now to the field of property, production, and private enterprise. It is clear from the text that property is privately owned and that individuals are free to buy and sell it as they wish, as far as governmental control is concerned. Along the same line, it is also clear that there is no regimentation of the economy or production and that free private enterprise or *laissez faire* exists. There are restrictions on property ownership, slave ownership, and the use of land, however, which are not mentioned in Ruth. These are detailed in Leviticus 25. There it is stated that on every seventh year the land shall lie idle, and on every fiftieth year the land shall lie idle and Israelite slaves shall go free. The Hebrews had permission from God to make slaves of the peoples of Canaan, but their fellow Israelites could not be brought into permanent bondage.

If a Hebrew man fell into slavery because of debt, he was to be freed during the year of jubilee; if a man was for some reason forced to sell his land to someone outside of his immediate family, the ownership of the land was to revert to its former proprietor during the fiftieth year. In other words, when a Hebrew bought a piece of land, it was really purchased on a lease basis for a period of not more than forty-nine years, and the price he paid for the property was determined by the nearness of the jubilee year. Finally, it is quite obvious from the Book of Ruth that the productive process was carried on by means of hand labor.

The question of management and labor relations is closely associated with the subjects of production and private enterprise. The kind of work being done in the Book of Ruth is agricultural. Seemingly there is a distinction between types of workers, because in Ruth 2:4 there is a mention of reapers (probably hired for a brief period of time only) and in 2:5 notice is taken of a servant (he is either hired as permanent help or is a slave). Relationships between management and labor are cordial, for Boaz and his workers greet one another in the name of the Lord in 2:4; workers obey Boaz in 2:15, 16; and Boaz works beside them in 3:2.

The last field of sociology discussed in the outline provided earlier in this chapter concerned itself with social institutions promoting richer living. The only one of these referred to in the Book of Ruth is that of religion. Religion permeates the whole of the Jewish *Weltanschauung* (philosophy, view of life); every phase of social relationship is enriched by God's presence. Family life, community life, and labor and management relations are all integrated from the standpoint of the centrality of God and religion in the affairs of men, and it was this factor that proved to be the chief cohesive element in society in a day when "there was no king in Israel and every man did that which was right in his own eyes."

TOPICS FOR FURTHER STUDY

1. The family in patriarchal society.
2. The social provisions of Hebrew law.
3. The effects of sin on social relations. Note in this con-

nection the reasons for which divorce was permitted in the Old Testament.

4. Status of women in various Biblical societies; note such types as Ruth and Naomi, Esther and Vashti, Lydia at Philippi, Sarah, Rebekah, Miriam, the ten virgins, the woman with the issue of blood, the mother of Zebedee's children, Peter's mother-in-law, Sapphira, Pilate's wife, Priscilla (wife of Aquila), and Lois and Eunice.

5. Social relationships of Ephesians 5:21-6:9 and Colossians 3:18-4:1.

6. A comparison of social relations of the millennial day with present conditions; note such passages as Isaiah 35 and Romans 8:22.

7. An analysis of the threats of Rabshakeh (Is. 36; II Kings 18, 19; II Chron. 32) from the standpoint of propaganda devices listed in this chapter.

8. Relative control of governments over their people — the Babylonians and Persians as seen in the Book of Daniel, the Judges and David and Solomon in relation to the Israelites, and the Egyptians to their subjects as portrayed in the Book of Exodus.

9. Slavery in the Bible. Consider such matters as the Hebrew slaves in Egypt and Babylon, Paul's attitude toward slavery as seen in Ephesians, Colossians, and Philemon, etc.

10. The poor in Scripture — provisions for the poor in Hebrew society; the poor in the Jerusalem Church; Paul's collection for the poor; Palestinian beggars mentioned in the Gospels, and the potter's field purchased with Judas' blood money.

BIBLIOGRAPHY

Barnes, Harry Elmer, Social Institutions (New York: Prentice-Hall, 1942).

Bogardus, Emory S., Sociology (New York: The Macmillan Co., 1950).

Gillin, John L., and John P. Gillin, Cultural Sociology (New York: The Macmillan Co., 1948).

Lee, Alfred M., ed., New Outline of the Principles of Sociology (New York: Barnes & Noble, 1946).

MacIver, R. M., and C. H. Page, Society: An Introductory Analysis (New York: Rinehart & Co., 1949).

Ogburn, William F., and M. F. Nimkoff, *Sociology* (New York: Houghton Mifflin, 1950).

Robinson, Thomas H., *et. al.*, *A Survey in the Social Sciences* (New York: Harper & Brothers, 1940).

Young, Kimball, *Sociology, A Study of Society and Culture* (New York: American Book Co., 1942).

CHAPTER XIII

THE POLITICAL METHOD

The political method of Bible study seeks to investigate all matters relating to the management of governmental affairs of nations mentioned in the Bible. Since political institutions of the Near East have been essentially despotic in nature from earliest times, it is not possible to organize our consideration according to categories familiar to students of American Government. Neither is it desired to be highly technical in our discussion of this branch of knowledge. In keeping with the approach of this present volume, which is to provide methods of Bible study usable by those who may not have received extensive formal education, a very simplified plan is sketched for this field of investigation. First of all the outline of procedure is detailed, after which a discussion and brief illustration of points in the outline are provided; then a fully developed example, a bibliography, and a word about topics for further study are furnished.

OUTLINE OF PROCEDURE

    I. Types of Government
   II. Philosophy of Government
  III. Geography of Government
       A. Area governed
       B. Organization of subdivisions
       C. Seats of government
       D. Influence of geography on government
   IV. Leaders in Government
    V. Functions of Government
       A. Varied civil administration
       B. Public finance

C. War and international relations
D. Judicial affairs
VI. Activities of Various Religious Groups and Leaders in Government

Types of Government. Although there are many kinds of governmental organization in the world, basically the types are three: unitary, federal, and confederate. In the unitary type, officers of the central government have complete control over local offices and officials, to the point of controverting decisions of lesser officeholders and even to the extent of removing them from their positions. Absolute monarchies and dictatorships are unitary in nature. For the most part, Near Eastern governments from Biblical times to the present have been of this character; democratic procedures and federalism have never gained much headway in the Middle East. The federal form of government, on the other hand, guarantees a certain amount of autonomy to local units; the latter are protected from too much control on the part of national officials by constitutional or legal processes; representative procedures are maintained. Confederation is the opposite of a unitary organization — the local units assert a supremacy over the central government, and a very loose sort of arrangement prevails. The Philistine pentapolis, the five cities of the Amorites, and the Israelites during the days of the Judges are good examples of Biblical confederacies.

Philosophy of government. Comprehended here are the issues of who is sovereign in the state and what is the source of government. In a democracy the people are sovereign; in a theocracy God, a god, or a religious body is in control; in an aristocracy or oligarchy a certain few wealthy and powerful individuals rule the state; in a dictatorship one individual exercises complete power over the citizenry and does not answer to the people for his acts. Nebuchadnezzar is a good example of one-man rule of a nation, while Samuel's ministry would be classified as theocratic in nature; the common people of Oriental nations rarely ever have much to say about their government.

The source of government or law is either human or divine.

It may be characteristic of Communistic or Fascistic leaders to claim that they have attained their high political position and formulated the policies of state by virtue of their own abilities and in defiance of the Almighty; and some of the kings of the Bible may have taken the same attitude; but most rulers of Bible times liked to think that their power came from deity. The divine-right-of-kings philosophy — that they were ordained to office by the Most High God or some petty god — was common in the ancient Eastern Mediterranean world. Furthermore, kings did not usually represent their legal systems as products of their own brains. For instance, when Hammurabi set up his famous code in Babylon, he had carved at the top of the stele on which it was inscribed a scene in which the god Shamash imparts the provisions of the code to him. In the case of spiritual leaders such as Moses, legal authority and leadership power actually did come from God; his was not merely an effort to gain prestige for himself and his program by attributing them to Jehovah.

Geography of government. In a discussion of the geography of government, we are concerned with government in relation to the area controlled. First of all, the boundaries of a territory should be delineated and the approximate size given, either in terms of square miles or in comparison with that of some modern state. Second, if the country is of any importance, there will be subdivisions for the sake of more efficient administration. In the Roman Empire of Paul's day, for instance, imperial holdings were divided into provinces, some of which were controlled by the senate and others by the emperor. Provinces such as Gaul, Spain, and Syria were not so thoroughly Romanized as the rest and therefore required a larger number of occupation troops; these were reserved by the emperor in order that he might maintain his grip on the military situation of the Empire. Macedonia, Africa, Asia, and others were pacified and were thus allocated to the senate for administration. The former were governed by propraetors and the latter by proconsuls. This distinction is borne out by such Biblical passages as Acts 13:7, where the ruler of Cyprus, a senatorial province, is described as a proconsul in the Greek. Third, it will be necessary to note seats of government, their location, size, and the relative importance of each to the affairs of state. For example, in New Testament times Palestine had two main centers of jurisdiction — Caesarea and Jerusalem. Caesarea, on the Mediterranean seacoast, had been chosen by the Romans as the civil capital; while the Jews still considered Jerusalem, up in the Judean highlands, as the seat of government, and it was as far as religious affairs were concerned. Even the Romans were obliged to maintain officials there. Last, it must be observed that geographical factors often influence politics greatly. Some geographers and historians go to extremes on this matter, however; the influence of geography must be classified more as a conditioning than a causative factor. That is to say, geography must not be looked upon as the sole cause of affairs as they are; rather it must be viewed as an element contributing in large or small measure to an existing situation. The fact that Palestine was a small strip of land wedged between great world empires greatly affected her national politics; the lack of good harbors along the Mediterranean coast of Palestine and the natural inclination of the people to pastoral and agrarian pursuits tended to restrict the activities of Jewish government to those matters during much of its history.

Leaders in government. Throughout the Bible political leaders are mentioned, either by name or the position they hold. Hosts of kings are listed, both for the nation of Israel and for powers surrounding Israel. There is a mention of presidents in Daniel 6:2; taskmasters are named in Exodus 1:11; in Acts 17:8 we read of rulers of the city (politarchs); Gallio, the deputy (proconsul) of Achaia, judged Paul in Acts 18:12-16. These and many more must be investigated as to the responsibility their position entailed and as to their personal lives and activity if one is to understand aright the politics of their respective nations. Not only will it be necessary to make a complete study of these individuals as they appear in Scripture, but extra-Biblical sources must be utilized as well.

Functions of government. National and local governments, whatever their type, are called upon to perform varied civil responsibilities for their people. The Pharaoh of Egypt found it necessary to develop a program of food procurement and storage in preparation for famine in the days of Joseph; the store cities of Pithom and Raamses were built by Israelite slaves in the Mosaic period; officials avidly sought out and trained future national leadership for Babylon when Daniel was a lad; the town clerk endeavored to maintain order in Ephesus (Acts 19: 35) when the guild of silversmiths stirred up a riot against Paul. A wide field of such miscellaneous services is engaged in by the governments of other nations described in the Bible, and a study of these activities will enhance our knowledge of the political context of the Biblical narrative.

Public finance is a major task of any government; and this issue, too, is of significance in the study of Scripture. The Jews resented Roman efforts to collect taxes in Palestine, and tax gatherers such as Levi the Publican were greatly disliked and considered as traitors to their people because they would consent to act as an agent for a foreign nation. The money question is also a primary issue in the military activities of Tiglath-pileser and Sennacherib of Assyria as they put Menahem of Israel and Hezekiah of Judah to tribute.

One of the biggest problems any nation has is getting along with its neighbors, and Biblical Palestine was no exception. It was in the unfortunate geographical position of constituting a bridge between two continents; as such it was an international football, kicked around between Egypt, Assyria, Babylon and Persia. The Biblical narrative is a continual recital of conflicting national interests and the wars which resulted over those issues.

Another important responsibility of government is the administration of judicial affairs. Rome dispensed her obligation to her citizens in this regard as she provided a Gallio in Corinth to adjudicate Paul's case there and as she permitted Paul to appeal to Caesar and then furnished his transportation to Rome; Persia fulfilled her duty to her subjects when Haman was hanged for his part in the vicious plot to exterminate the Jews; tiny Bethlehem took care of her legal matters through the in-

strumentality of a group of town elders that met at the gate in
Ruth's lifetime.

Often the judicial provisions and attitudes of a people can
best be discovered through an evaluation of their law codes.
The Jews had the Mosaic code; the Babylonians had the Hammurabi and Lipit Ishtar codes; the Assyrians and Hittites also
constructed law codes. These are all available to the student
in part or *in toto;* partial translations of many of these works
appear in the back of George Barton's *Archaeology and the
Bible.*

Religion in government. Often religious leaders and groups
play a very important part in political affairs. The Scribes,
Pharisees, and Sanhedrin in New Testament Palestine, the
priests of Dagon in Philistia, the priests of Baal in Israel, and
the court priests at the palace of Nebuchadnezzar all had their
part to play in the government of their respective countries.
Religion, whether pagan or Christian, made just as great an
impact on ancient society as it does on that of today.

DEVELOPMENT OF EXAMPLE

It now remains to demonstrate by way of example how this
method works. Babylon in the days of Nebuchadnezzar has
been chosen to accomplish the purpose. The terminology assigned by historians and archeologists to this general time is
the Neo-Babylonian Empire, which begins with the fall of Nineveh in 612 B.C. and ends with the fall of Babylon in 539 B.C.
Let us, then, proceed with the discussion of this empire according to the outline that has just been set forth.

As is customary among the nations of Biblical lands, Babylon has a unitary type of government; the decrees of the king
are law throughout the empire. This is obvious from such
passages as Daniel 3, where the entire populace of the domain
is commanded to bow down before the image which Nebuchadnezzar has erected; if the ruler is able to harness his subjects
to cater to a whim of this nature, it should not take much imagination to see how completely he controlled all the affairs of
state. His iron grip is further demonstrated in the decree of
destruction which he hurled at those who should blaspheme the

God of Shadrach, Meshach, and Abed-nego (Dan. 3:29), and in the evaluation of Nebuchadnezzar's power by Daniel (5:19).

Regarding the Babylonian philosophy of government, it may be said that sovereignty in the state lies with the king who possesses dictatorial powers; such is the conclusion one draws from evidence of the nature presented in the foregoing paragraph. The source of power and authority in government was felt by most Chaldean rulers to be their own personal strength and ability, though they frequently made claims that one or the other of the gods had endowed them with their position. Nebuchadnezzar shared this attitude during the early years of his reign, for Daniel 4:30 reads, "Is not this great Babylon, which I have built for the royal dwelling-place by the might of my power and for the glory of my majesty?" God smote him with insanity, however, until he was stripped of his pride; then his philosophy of power and sovereignty was changed, as is represented by his words, "I blessed the Most High, and I praised and honored him that liveth for ever; for his dominion is an everlasting dominion, and his kingdom from generation to generation . . . and he doeth according to his will in the army of heaven, and among the inhabitants of the earth; and none can stay his hand . . ." (Dan. 4:34, 35). It is interesting to observe, however, that Daniel had this view of Nebuchadnezzar's rule from the beginning; he declares in the interpretation of the forgotten dream, "Thou, O king, art a king of kings, unto whom the God of heaven hath given the kingdom, the power, and the strength, and the glory" (Dan. 2:37).

The geography of government next demands our attention. Babylonia proper was only about the size of New Jersey, but during the period under consideration, it came to control by means of conquest Assyria, Syria, Palestine, and much of the Arabian Desert. Naturally, the occupation of this vast area gave the Chaldeans a number of important cities which might serve as administrative centers — Nineveh, Tyre, Sidon, Damascus, etc. — but Babylon is the only one mentioned in this connection in Scripture; so our interest will be centered there. The city was massively fortified with walls and towers and entered through the famous Ishtar Gate. Ancient commentators disagree somewhat on the size and length of the walls, but it may be safe to say that the circumference was some forty or fifty miles. The ruins even today spread for many miles along both sides of the Euphrates River. The city was laid out in a rather orderly fashion with streets intersecting at right angles. Not much is known about the provincial organization of the Babylonian Empire, but certainly a territory of such great magnitude had some sort of subdivisions. This fact is intimated in Daniel 2:48, 49, where Daniel is made ruler over the province of Babylon; in II Kings 25:22, where Gedaliah was appointed governor over the territory of Judea after it capitulated to Nebuchadnezzar; and in Daniel 3:3, where there is specific mention of "rulers of provinces."

Geographical features greatly affected the political life of Babylonia in that the alluvial soil, without natural barriers and bordered by mountains supporting a hardy people, was a constant scene of invasion, the result of which was frequent change of overlords as well as influx of new racial strains. Moreover, the people were dependent for livelihood upon the Tigris and Euphrates Rivers, which were tapped for the irrigation of the soil. Close cooperation among the populace and effective governmental supervision were needed to preserve this irrigation network in order to sustain physical life.

The rulers of the Neo-Babylonian Empire were seven in number. Nabopolassar (626-605) engineered a successful revolt in the province of Babylon against Assyrian overlords and took the city of Nineveh in 612 B.C. He was followed by Nebuchadnezzar (605-562), who was the chief builder of the empire and most famous ruler of the period. He fortified Babylon and built the famous hanging gardens, conquered Tyre and Sidon and the Jews, and extended the power of the Chaldeans into the Arabian Desert. His successors had little of the political and military genius which characterized his forty-three year reign.

After Nebuchadnezzar's death, the government fell into the hands of his unworthy son Amel-Marduk (Evil-Merodach, II Kings 25:27). The priestly class soon wearied of the unspeakable misrule of this court weakling and were a party to his assassination about three years later. Neriglissar (Nergalsharezer of Jeremiah 39:3), brother-in-law of Evil-Merodach, took the throne in 559. He was fairly successful in ruling the nation but died in 555, leaving the reins of government to his young son, Labashi-Marduk. Almost at once plots were initiated to take the life of this lad. Superficial reasons for disposing of him included such things as a display of evil traits of character. Labashi-Marduk lasted only nine months. His successor was Nabonidus, of the priestly class, not at all related to the reigning house. He made his son, Belshazzar, co-ruler with him; and it was Belshazzar who exercised regal authority in the capital at the time Cyrus brought about the fall of the Neo-Babylonian Empire.

Scripture records many other Babylonian officials in addition to the kings; in Daniel we read of the prince of the eunuchs, Arioch, the captain of the King's guard, governors over the wise men of Babylon, princes, judges, treasurers, counselors, sheriffs, and lords. The occupations of most of these men should be obvious, but some explanation might be given of the terms "eunuch" and "sheriff." The former was an emasculated male employed in Oriental harems as bedroom attendants or sometimes as trusted public officials; the latter is the translation of a term of uncertain meaning but thought to be a kind of lawyer or legal advisor.

It may be supposed that the Babylonian government performed all the usual functions of government, but there are specific indications in Scriptures as to its activity. Nebuchadnezzar was a great builder, a fact which is confirmed by Scripture (Dan. 4:30) and archeological sources; the mention of treasurers in Daniel 3:3 demonstrates activity in public finance; the listing of judges and sheriffs in Daniel 3:3, and the assignment of Daniel and others to rule over provinces shows that there was provision for judicial machinery. Probably the code of Hammurabi, though promulgated about 1700 B.C., remained as a basis for much of the legal development of Babylonia in 600. A translation and discussion of this code is found in Barton, *Archaeology and the Bible,* pages 378-406. These 282 laws deal with such important issues as assault and battery, slaves, marriage, robbery, real estate, straying of livestock, farming, and rents and prices. The fact that there were regularly appointed counselors seems to indicate that the king had some sort of council or cabinet possessing a certain amount of authority in government. The military activity of the Babylonians pervades many passages in the Prophets and historical books. Ample provision was made by the king and his advisors for the development of a strong military machine. The foreign policy was aggressive, at least in Nebuchadnezzar's day, when Palestine and Syria were taken; and possibly there was an invasion of Egypt. A continuation of the Assyrian deportation policy was utilized in dealing with conquered peoples, for many of the inhabitants of Palestine were removed to Mesopotamia, and into Palestine were brought others who would not be expected to revolt.

That religious groups and individuals were influential in the Babylonian government has already been noted in that priests were a party to the assassination of the Biblical Nergalsharezer, and a priest by the name of Nabonidus was co-ruler at the time of the fall of Babylon. But this information is gained from secular sources; the Bible also gives some intimations along the same line. Nebuchadnezzar placed great confidence in the magicians and astrologers when he desired to learn the interpretation of his dream (Dan. 2:10); Belshazzar also called upon this group when he wanted to know the interpretation of the handwriting on the wall. The fact that these priestly officials were unable to satisfy the king on either occasion does not lessen the indication of their influence in the state; for if they had been able to interpret the dream or handwriting in any intelligent way whatsoever, the king would have listened to them and their power over public policies issuing from such interpretations would have been tremendous. Since they were summoned on these occasions, we may take it that they had been called on before and had fulfilled their responsibility at such times. In this same regard it may be added that Daniel was something of a religious official himself — at least he became such on occasion — and it was for his religious service that he was rewarded by Nebuchadnezzar and Belshazzar.

It is true that Babylon in her heyday was a great political power, and at least during the rule of Nebuchadnezzar she boasted an efficient governmental machinery; but her moral fiber was weak and it was in the midst of drunken revelry and mockery of the Most High God on the part of the leaders of state that Cyrus the Persian marched into the capital and the death knell of empire was sounded.

SUGGESTIONS FOR FURTHER STUDY

Scripture is replete with references to nations of the Near East, but few of these are sufficiently discussed in the Bible or sufficiently known by means of historical or archeological investigation to permit their study from the standpoint of the political method of Bible study. Nations which may be considered by means of this approach, however, are Assyria, Babylon, Egypt, Hittites, Israel, Judah, Persia, Philistia, Phoenicia, and Rome.

BIBLIOGRAPHY

In addition to such basic works as the *Encyclopaedia Britannica, Americana Encyclopedia, Encyclopedia of the Social Sciences, The New Schaff-Herzog Encyclopedia of Religious Knowledge,* the *International Standard Bible Encyclopedia,* and *Hastings' Dictionary of the Bible,* the following books will prove to be helpful in developing the political method of Bible study.

Adams, J. M., *Ancient Records and the Bible* (Nashville: Broadman Press, 1946).

Barton, George A., *Archaeology and the Bible* (7th ed.; Philadelphia: American Sunday-School Union, 1937).

Breasted, James Henry, *A History of Egypt* (New York: Charles Scribner's Sons, 1909).

Finegan, Jack, *Light from the Ancient Past* (Princeton: Princeton University Press, 1946).

Hurlbut, Jesse Lyman, *A Bible Atlas* (New York: Rand McNally & Co., 1910).

Miller, Madeleine S., and J. Lane, *Harper's Bible Dictionary* (New York: Harper & Brothers, 1952).

Olmstead, A. T., *History of Assyria* (New York: Charles Scribner's Sons, 1923).

————, *History of Palestine and Syria* (New York: Charles Scribner's Sons, 1931).

————, *History of the Persian Empire* (Chicago: University of Chicago Press, 1948).

Steindorff, George, and Keith C. Seele, *When Egypt Ruled the East* (Chicago: University of Chicago Press, 1942).

Wright, George E., and Floyd V. Filson, *The Westminster Historical Atlas to the Bible* (Philadelphia: The Westminster Press, 1946).

CHAPTER XIV

THE CULTURAL METHOD

Our English word *culture* comes from the Latin *cultura,* meaning *till* or *cultivate.* By implication the root provides a picture of a farmer tilling, as it were, the soil of the mind, planting there intellectual seed, fertilizing it, and cultivating it often so the plant may not be stunted by a hard crust of intellectual disinterest, until it may be said that the individual has become *cultured.* Culture comes to mean, then, enlightenment and refinement of the moral, intellectual, and social nature by means of mental and aesthetic training. Culture is often confused with civilization, but the latter applies to human society and designates an advanced state of material and social well being, whereas culture is the intellectual content of that civilization.

The cultural content of civilization is comprehended under the headings of religion, science, music, art, architecture, literature, and language. Since whole chapters of this book are devoted both to the theological and the scientific methods of Bible study, these methods are omitted from the present consideration. For each of the other fields a brief series of questions or outline points is listed in order to furnish the student with something of a plan for investigating these subjects.

Music. Probably the first question that would be raised in speaking of music is, What did it sound like? Then there would be interest in the kind of instruments used, the place that vocal music played in the life of a given people, the way in which the musical program of a nation was influenced by that of surrounding nations, the types of music employed,

133

and the importance of the study of music to a better understanding of Scripture. Hebrew music as it existed up to the
time of the exile is discussed later in the chapter by way of
example of the cultural method.

Art. Various questions arise also in a consideration of the
art of people of the Bible. Naturally we would inquire first
into the nature of their artistic endeavor. Did they carve
statues in the round or chisel out bas reliefs? Were they
given to painting and fresco production? What can be said
about handcrafts such as jewelry, pottery, furniture making,
and embellishment of cloth? We might also demonstrate an
interest in the subjects represented in the artistic motif. Did
they utilize geometric designs or did they focus their attention
on people, animals and hunting scenes, war scenes, deities,
and the like? Then there arises the issue of whether or not
any prohibitions were placed upon their art by God. This
is a matter which affects Hebrew art to a great degree. In
Exodus 20:4 appears the statement, "Thou shalt not make
unto thee any graven image, or any likeness of any thing that
is in heaven above, or that is in the earth beneath, or that
is in the water under the earth." Obviously, all types of
sculpture would be included in this commandment; and the
Hebrews extended it to painting, pottery motifs, and other
types of decorative art. In fact, it may be said that for this
reason Jews of the Biblical period were not especially skilled
in many of the arts nor were they particularly interested in
them. One should not come to the conclusion, however, that
there was no Hebrew art; their aesthetic inclinations were
expressed more in the direction of music, literature, and jewelry
manufacture. Prohibitions did not curb the artistic endeavor
of nations surrounding Israel, and remains of their culture
provide a more fruitful study in this regard.

Another important facet of the study of art concerns influences which are brought to bear on its development in a
given nation. The consideration of the cultural synchronisms
of the Near East is a vast and interesting one but hardly
within the scope of this present work. Let it suffice, by way
of illustration, to say that Hebrew art was greatly influenced

by that of Phoenicia and to some extent by that of Egypt. For the construction of the temple Solomon hired Tyrian artisans skilled in the preparation of decorative fabrics and the production of art metal work; the "bell and pomegranate" figure, on the other hand, strongly resembles the Egyptian lotus-and-bud motif. A further word on this subject concerns its importance to Bible study. This should be obvious from what has already been said about Hebrew art, but it might be added that a clear understanding and visualization of the temple, tabernacle, and many other institutions and aspects of Biblical life is difficult without a serious investigation of the art of Biblical times.

Architecture. Many of the same questions raised in the foregoing study are apropos in respect to a discussion of Biblical architecture, but this inquiry takes a slightly different turn. A logical place to begin is with the types and magnitude of Biblical architecture. The temple, tabernacle, city walls and gates, palaces of such rulers as Ahab and Solomon, and Solomon's fortress cities and stables are a few of the structures mentioned in Scripture. The style of construction and the kind and source of materials used in building also must be considered. Just as in the study of art, so here influences brought to bear on architecture of Biblical peoples provide an interesting angle of investigation. This is especially true in the case of the Hebrews who during the Davidic and Solomonic days and in the Kingdom of Israel during the divided monarchy, employed Phoenician craftsmen for various phases of architectural construction, including the building of Solomon's navy. As this type of investigation progresses, its importance to Scripture will become obvious, for much of the context of the Biblical narrative will be seen more clearly; and the message of the Bible will take on new significance.

Literature and language. The Bible intimates or clearly speaks of quite a number of languages; among these are Hebrew, Aramaic, Egyptian, Babylonian, Assyrian, Hittite, Greek, Arabian and Canaanite dialects, and Persian. The student should endeavor to discover the nature of these languages —

whether they are alphabetic, syllabic, pictographic, etc. — and something of their origin. Then he will be interested in the types of literature produced by these ancient peoples, the extent of such literature, the influences or events which affected or produced these literary works, and the ways in which they influenced other literature or the progress of history. Consider, for instance, the effect which Mosaic legislation had upon the life and development of Israel or the impact such imperial decrees as that of Cyrus (as recorded in Ezra 1) had in respect to the restoration of the Hebrew Commonwealth.

In order that the student may more clearly discern the procedure and possibilities of the cultural method of Bible study, an example of the method is furnished by means of an outline of Hebrew music from early times to about 550 B.C.

THE MUSIC OF ISRAEL

Nature of Hebrew music. In Israel, music was important alike at home, in social gatherings, and in the field. It certainly was not all sacred but contributed to every activity of life, such as weddings and village feasts. David, however, is given the credit for making song and stringed music an integral part of the regular worship. He appointed four thousand to praise the Lord with instruments (I Chron. 23:5), and a total of 288 were instructed and cunning in the songs of the Lord (I Chron. 25:7).

It is hard to determine the nature of the Hebrew scale or the sounds emitted by their instruments. Burrows observes, "If architecture is frozen music, music may be called fluid architecture, much too fluid to be preserved in the earth like bricks and stone."[1] It is possible that their scale was pentatonic, but their music was probably modal. The Hebrews never invented a system of notation, so we have none of their melodies, such as those which are known to exist from titles of the Psalms.[2] For the same reason we can know nothing of their harmony. Perhaps their singing, as well as the accompaniment, was performed in unison.

---

[1] Millar Burrows, *What Mean These Stones?* (New Haven: American Schools of Oriental Research, 1941), p. 195.
[2] See the discussion in this chapter on Hebrew vocal music.

Instrumental music. There are thirteen musical instruments mentioned in the Old Testament (in the period prior to 550 B.C., which is as far as this study goes), including strings, wood-winds, and percussion. A listing and definition of these instruments is provided; for the convenience of the reader, the transliteration of Hebrew words is that which appears in Young's *Analytical Concordance.*

a. Stringed Instruments

'Asor (translated 3 times as "instrument of ten strings"; once as "ten"; 12 times as "tenth"). Some take this to be another term for a ten-stringed harp, and others feel that it is an instrument of some other nature, such as a zither.

Kinnor ("harp," 42 times). The *kinnor* is a lyre and not a harp. It must be noted, then, that David did not play a harp at all but a lyre, and wherever the word "harp" appears in the Old Testament it should be translated "lyre." We do not have much information about this instrument from the Old Testament, but other sources show that it was made of wood with gut or metal strings and was decorated variously. Its sound box was below, and a plectrum was generally used to play it.

Nebel ("psaltery," 23 times; "viol," 4). This is the true harp, a stringed instrument triangular in shape, with a resonance frame which slopes upward from the base; it is not played with a plectrum.

b. Wind Instruments

Chalil ("pipe," 6 times). Modern translators generally take this instrument to be a flute, but it is not absolutely certain whether it is the single or double flute.

Chatsotserah ("trumpet," 28 times; "trumpeter," 1). There is no particular problem in the identification of this instrument. It is the silver trumpet which God commanded Moses to make (Num. 10:2). Josephus describes it as nearly a yard long, a little wider than a flute, with a bell-like end, and a slight expansion at the mouthpiece to catch the breath.

Shophar ("cornet," 4 times; "trumpet," 68; taken to be synonymous with *qeren,* "horn," 75 times). This was originally a ram's horn in its natural form; then it was heated and flattened and bent to form a right angle. A skilled performer

138 EFFECTIVE BIBLE STUDY

could get several tones on it, but usually one got two — the tonic and the fifth. In later times these horns were made of metal and straightened, leading to confusion with the *chatsotserah*. The tone secured from a ram's horn would be loud and piercing and unsuited for concert music.

Ugab ("organ," 4 times). The identification in this case is uncertain. The *ugab* may have been a type of mouth organ or pan's pipe or possibly a kind of flute.

c. Percussion Instruments

Menaanim ("cornets," 1 time). This is probably the sistrum; this instrument had an oval frame, with iron rods having hooked ends lying loosely in holes in sides of the frame, to which a handle is attached.

Metsiltayim ("cymbals," 13 times). The evidence seems to point to the fact that this cymbal is like the one used in modern orchestras and bands, a plate-like affair that is clashed horizontally.

Paamon ("bell," 7 times). This term needs no particular comment; it was the bell that was sewed to the hem of the garment of the high priest.

Toph ("tabret," 8 times; "timbrel," 9). The *toph* was the instrument played by Miriam and the other women in Exodus 15:20. Scriptural references show that women usually played it, but men were not excluded (I Sam. 10:5). The *toph* is probably to be identified with the modern tambourine.

Shalishim ("instrument of music," 1 time). Some feel that this is the triangle, but there is no general agreement at the present time as to its nature.

Tseltselim ("cymbals," 3 times). These instruments are probably the conical type of cymbal known in Egypt and Assyria. They were struck together vertically.

Vocal music. There is very little light that can be shed upon the vocal music of Israel, but it is evident from such passages as Exodus 15:20ff. that the favorite style was antiphonal.[3] This kind of singing was done responsively, and it might be executed in one of three ways: with a leader and choir, a choir and congregation, or two choirs. Musical instru-

[3] Psalm 136 is an excellent example of an antiphonal Psalm.

ments were used for the purpose of accompanying singers, and not for the sake of orchestras as such. It is entirely possible, as some suggest, that the word *selah* which appears so often in the Psalms was a pause in the vocal part while an interlude or finale was rendered.

Indications which may be gleaned from titles of the Psalms reflect something of the high development of Hebrew vocal music. Apparently many of them are instructions telling how the Psalms should be sung. While there is some difference of opinion on this subject, it is likely that the following suggestions are near to the truth. The translators of the American Standard Version apparently felt so.

1. The title of Psalm 4 in the King James Version reads, "To the chief Musician on Neginoth." Render the last word "stringed instruments" or "string music."

2. *Nehiloth* in the title of Psalm 5 probably should be translated "wind instruments."

3. In the King James Version, the title of Psalm 6 reads, "To the chief Musician on Neginoth upon Sheminith." This might better be expressed, "To the chief Musician with string music in the eighth mode."

4. No doubt the practice of putting religious words to secular tunes was prevalent even in ancient times because some of the titles give instructions that the Psalm is to be sung to a certain tune. For example, Psalm 22 is to be sung to the tune of "The Hind of the Dawn" or "The Hind of the Morning"; Psalm 45 is supposed to be sung to the tune of "The Lilies."

From this brief development of Hebrew music, it should be obvious that there is real value in the cultural method of Bible study. If the student is interested in pursuing the subject of music further, he may do so with the aid of the bibliography listed at the end of this chapter. Helps are also suggested for the study of language, literature, art and architecture.

SUGGESTIONS FOR FURTHER BIBLE STUDY

1. Architecture of the temple.
2. Artistry of the tabernacle.

3. Professions and trades of the Bible.
4. Wearing apparel of the Bible.
5. Jewelry of the Bible and divine attitudes toward it.
6. The origin and development of alphabetic writing in Palestine and the rest of the Near East.
7. A study of Baal worship or the religion of Egypt, with a consideration of effects on Hebrew worship.

BIBLIOGRAPHY

A. ART AND ARCHITECTURE

Burrows, Millar, *What Mean These Stones?* (New Haven: American Schools of Oriental Research, 1941).

Caldecott, W. S., and James Orr, "Temple," *International Standard Bible Encyclopedia,* V, 230-40.

Dalman, G., "Synagogue," *The New Schaff-Herzog Encyclopedia of Religious Knowledge,* XI, 213-16.

Dickie, A. C., "Architecture," *International Standard Bible Encyclopedia,* I, 234-38.

Finegan, Jack, *Light from the Ancient Past* (Princeton: Princeton University Press, 1946).

Gilmore, George W., "Temples, Hebrew," *The New Schaff-Herzog Encyclopedia of Religious Knowledge,* XI, 293-96.

International Standard Bible Encyclopedia, "General Index," list of articles under "Architecture," p. 3184, and under "Crafts," pp. 3217-8.

Kennedy, A. R. S., "Arts and Crafts," in James Hastings, ed., *Dictionary of the Bible,* Special Illustrated Edition, pp. 52-54.

Miller, Madeleine S., and J. Lane, *Encyclopedia of Bible Life,* articles on "Arts and Crafts," "Apparel," "Jewelry," "Professions and Trades" (New York: Harper & Brothers, 1944).

————, *Harper's Bible Dictionary,* articles on "Architecture," "Jewelry," "Synagogue," and "Temple" (New York: Harper & Brothers, 1952).

B. LANGUAGES AND LITERATURE

Buhl, F., "Hebrew Language and Literature," *The New Schaff-Herzog Encyclopedia of Religious Knowledge,* V, 183-92.

Gelb, I. J., *A Study of Writing* (Chicago: University of Chicago Press, 1952).

Miller, Madeleine S., and J. Lane, *Harper's Bible Dictionary,* articles on "Languages" and "Writing" (New York: Harper & Brothers, 1952).

Richardson, E. C., "Writing," *International Standard Bible Encyclopedia,* V, 3114-26.

Robertson, A. T., "Language of the New Testament," *International Standard Bible Encyclopedia,* III, 1826-32.

Unger, Merrill F., *Introductory Guide to the Old Testament* (Grand Rapids: Zondervan Publishing House, 1951), pp. 116-24.

Weir, Thomas W., "Languages of the Old Testament," *International Standard Bible Encyclopedia*, III, 1832-36.

C. Music

Benzinger, I., "Sacred Music: Hebrew," *The New Schaff-Herzog Encyclopedia of Religious Knowledge*, X, 148-52.

LaViolette, Wesley, *Music and Its Makers* (Chicago: University of Knowledge, Inc., 1938).

Millar, James, "Music," *International Standard Bible Encyclopedia*, III, 2094-2101.

Miller, Madeleine S., and J. Lane, "Music," *Harper's Bible Dictionary* (New York: Harper & Brothers, 1952), pp. 466-70.

————, "Musical Instruments," *Encyclopedia of Bible Life* (New York: Harper & Brothers, 1944), pp. 284-98.

Prince, J. D., "Music," *Encyclopaedia Biblica*, III.

Sachs, Curt, *The History of Musical Instruments* (New York: W. W. Norton & Co., 1940).

Sellers, O. R., "Musical Instruments of Israel," *Biblical Archaeologist*, September, 1941.

Vos, Howard F., "The Music of Israel," *Bibliotheca Sacra*, October, 1949, pp. 446-57, and January, 1950, pp. 64-70.

Chapter XV

THE SCIENTIFIC METHOD

Science is a term which is used in such a wide variety of ways that it is often difficult to ascertain the connotation which a writer or speaker attaches to it. We hear of mental science or psychology; moral science or ethics; pure science, consisting of mathematics as opposed to natural or physical science, which rests on observation and experiment; applied science — the findings of science applied to everyday life; natural or physical sciences, which include biology, chemistry, geology, mathematics, physics, and astronomy; and social sciences, which deal with human relationships and include sociology, history, politics, and anthropology. Of course, others use such terminology as the "scientific approach" and the "scientific viewpoint." Generally speaking, however, a science is a branch of study concerned with the observation and classification of facts in an effort to establish certain verifiable general laws; and the scientific method is the amassing, testing, coordinating, and systematizing of knowledge.

Attention is centered in this chapter on the physical sciences, since chapters have already been devoted to sociology, politics, and history; and others will be given over to the study of philosophy and psychology. Of the physical sciences emphasis is placed on zoology, botany, and mineralogy (this is a branch of the field of geology; matters of land configuration, etc., have already been considered in Chapter XI). Zoology deals with the animal kingdom, while botany concerns itself with plant life, and mineralogy has to do with mineral substances. One could study the Bible from the standpoint of chemistry, mathematics, physics, and astronomy; but since these investigations require a fairly extensive technical knowledge on the part of the reader, they do not fall within the scope of this work.

Development of Method

It almost goes without saying that the scientific method of Bible study does not involve the microscope and the test tube; it is scientific in that it comprehends an investigation of Biblical objects and organisms which are classified in the secular world according to various branches of scientific knowledge. In developing this method, a fairly simple procedure may be employed. The following is offered as a guide.

1. List the name of the animal, plant, or mineral as it appears in a given verse in the version you are using.

2. Look at other versions to ascertain if the translation there is the same as in the version with which you began.

3. Next go to Bible dictionaries and encyclopedias to discover exactly what kind of species you are studying.

4. Look at all the places where this plant, animal, or mineral appears in Scripture and try to learn if the name is ever used in a figurative or symbolical sense. For instance, in Daniel 2, gold, silver, and iron are made symbolic; in chapters seven and eight, a lion, bear, leopard, ram, and goat are declared to represent world empires or rulers.

5. What special significance does the mention of the object or organism have in any particular Biblical reference? What importance may be attached to the combinations of animals, etc., which appear in various passages? For example, in Isaiah 11, several ferocious animals are paired off with their natural prey in an effort to demonstrate the revolution in nature which will take place during the days of the millennial kingdom.

6. Now collect all the information concerning an animal, plant, or mineral from passages where the name appears, in an effort to determine what the Bible teaches about it.

7. Last, try to discover what characteristics of a biological or mineral specimen may be used to illustrate Christian truth. Good examples of this type of study are found in the parable

of the shepherd and the sheep (John 10) and the account of the vine and the branches (John 15).

EXAMPLE OF METHOD

To illustrate how one might develop this method of Bible study, ten selections have been made at random from the plant, animal, bird, and insect worlds. The study of each roughly follows the sevenfold plan outlined above. This material could very conveniently be charted by the student in parallel columns on large sheets of paper, but it is more easily put into paragraph form here.

Cummin. This word is translated the same in the King James and American Standard Versions. It is a flowering plant valued for its seeds (resembling caraway seeds) which are used as spice in bread and meat and as a medicine. In the two passages where the term appears (Is. 28:25-27; Matt. 23:23) no figurative or symbolical sense is intended; but a spiritual principle is involved in the Matthew reference, where Jesus condemns the scribes and Pharisees for tithing these inconsequential seeds and leaving important things undone. About all that can be learned about this plant from Scripture is that it was a cultivated one rather than wild and that it was beaten out with a rod when threshing time came.

Mustard. In all five occurrences of this word in the New Testament it is translated the same in the American Standard and King James Versions. The American and Palestinian varieties of mustard are much the same, with the exception that in Palestine the mustard plant sometimes grows to a height of twelve feet. This plant is used by our Lord to illustrate teachings concerning the Kingdom and faith. The small beginnings of the Kingdom are indicated by the insignificant seed. In fact, little is expected of it; but contrary to expectations, it becomes a great institution just as the mustard seed develops into a good sized tree. The same juxtaposition of small and great is developed by Jesus when He states that if men will have faith to the extent of a grain of mustard seed, they may move mountains.

Gopher. Gopher wood is mentioned only once in the Bible,

Genesis 6:14, where it is noted that this is the type of wood from which the ark constructed by Noah was made. Both the King James and American Standard Versions translate it the same. Identification is rather uncertain, but many commentators feel that it is cypress; others say that it is possibly of the pine family.

Shittah (sing.); *Shittim* (pl). This kind of wood is mentioned a total of twenty-eight times in Scripture, all of which appear in Exodus, with the exception of the Deuteronomy 10:3 and Isaiah 41:19 references. The King James Version always speaks of this type of wood as *shittim*, while the American Standard uniformly translates the term *acacia*. Botanists have identified the tree as the desert acacia, which has hard orange-toned branches, produces feathery flowers, and even in barren areas grows to a height of twenty feet. Acacia wood was used in construction of the tabernacle and its furniture.

Fox. All nine occurrences of this word are translated *fox* both in the King James and American Standard Versions. The Hebrew term covers both jackal and fox, and the *Harper's Bible Dictionary* suggests that *jackal* is preferable in Judges 15:4, Psalm 63:10, and Nehemiah 4:3.[1] In those cases the same recommendation is made in the marginal references of the American Standard Version. If the three references listed above be reserved for a description of jackals, the remaining passages where foxes are mentioned teach that they live in holes in the ground, haunt deserted ruins, are cunning marauders and are known for slyness. In a metaphorical figure, Jesus compared Herod to a fox in Luke 13:32; in Matthew 8:20, He made it clear to His followers that the foxes who have holes in the earth for dwelling places have a more certain abode than the Son of Man and His followers. The Lamentations 5:18 reference indicates that Jerusalem is such a complete desolation that it has become a habitation of foxes.

Ass. This term, a translation of five Hebrew and two Greek words, is rendered the same in the King James and American Standard Versions. The Oriental ass is very different from the

[1] Madeleine S. and J. Lane Miller, *Harper's Bible Dictionary* (New York: Harper & Brothers, 1952), p. 207.

Occidental. It is related to the zebra and is usually reddish brown in color, but a few are white. It is known for its patience, submissiveness, and intelligence, whereas the Western ass is proverbially known as stupid and stubborn. The ass appears as the symbol of Issachar (Gen. 49:14), a willing burden-bearer. There is a host of references in Scripture to the ass; some of these merely describe the animal, and others illustrate religious truth. The ass, as well as his master, was to rest on the Sabbath (Ex. 23:12); the firstling was to be redeemed; it served as a beast of burden (I Sam. 16:20) and a means of transportation (Judg. 10:4); and it was not to be unequally yoked with an ox (Deut. 22:10). Israel was re-proved (Is. 1:3) because she did not give allegiance to her master, and the ass had more sense than that. The ass was an animal that symbolized peace, humility, and, white asses, royalty (Judg. 5:10). The fact that Jesus rode on an ass, which was probably white, at once denoted His humility and royalty (Zech. 9:9; Matt. 21:5).

Goat. The various versions agree in the translation of this term. Regarding identification, it may be said that the goat mentioned in Scripture is possibly like the goat with which we are familiar; it is similar to the sheep but different in that the male goat is bearded and the ram is not. Its horns are differ-ent from the ram's and its odor stronger than that of a sheep. It is not improbable that some species of an ibex is denoted in a few references. This animal is used symbolically of evil individuals in Matthew 25:32, 33 and of the king of Greece in Daniel 8. Biblical references to the goat demonstrate that it was of importance as a sin offering and as a scape goat on the Day of Atonement, in providing part of the tent covering for the tabernacle, and in supplying milk, food, and clothing.

Quail. The word is translated uniformly in the various ver-sions. This bird is to be identified with the common quail of the present day. The only time that it figures in Scripture is during the desert wanderings of the Israelites, when it pro-vided variety in their diet and on one occasion (Num. 11:33) became a plague to them because of their disobedience to God.

Sparrow. The word *sparrow* is a translation of the Hebrew *tzippor*, which seems to have been a generic name for all small birds of sparrow-like species that frequent house and garden. Of the more than forty occurrences of this word in the Old Testament, few are rendered *sparrow*; most are translated *bird* or *fowl*. The Greek *strouthion* occurs twice in the New Testament (Matt. 10:29; Luke 12:6, 7) and is translated *sparrow* in both cases. Sparrows are referred to in English versions to illustrate the care of the Father and the poignant sorrow of the Psalmist. In the first instance, Jesus makes it clear (Matt. 10:29-31) that since the Father is interested in every insignificant sparrow, certainly He is infinitely more concerned about His spiritual children. In Psalm 102:7, the sacred writer illustrates his grief by saying, "I watch, and am become like a sparrow that is alone upon the housetop." The depth of his sorrow and loneliness is better understood when one remembers that the sparrow always travels in chattering groups.

Locust. This is the rendering in a number of English versions for several Hebrew words and one Greek term for certain species of grasshoppers destructive of vegetation. These grasshoppers are usually referred to as a destructive plague, and in the Book of Joel they are figurative of an advancing army of men. They became a plague to Pharaoh during the days of Moses' pleading; God threatened Israel with them as a result of the latter's disobedience (Deut. 28:42; Joel 1-4; Nahum 3:15-17). The Psalmist compared his experience to that of the locust when he said, "I am tossed up and down as the locust" (Ps. 109:23). The meaning of this passage is that the writer is as weak and powerless as a swarm of locusts driven by the wind. Locusts were not forbidden food for the Israelites, and they were part of the diet of John the Baptist (Matt. 3:4; Mark 1:6).

It should be obvious from this brief treatment of these species selected from the world of nature that the scientific method can greatly enhance one's understanding and appreciation of Scripture. May the reader, then, stop to investigate the birds, animals, insects, fish, plants, trees, and minerals which he meets as he studies his Bible.

BIBLIOGRAPHY

Hastings' *Dictionary of the Bible* (London: T. & T. Clark, 1910), 5 volumes.

The International Standard Bible Encyclopedia (Grand Rapids: Wm. B. Eerdmans Publishing Co., 1943), 5 volumes.

Miller, Madeleine S., and J. Lane, *Encyclopedia of Bible Life* (New York: Harper & Brothers, 1944).

————, *Harpers Bible Dictionary* (New York: Harper & Brothers, 1952).

The New Schaff-Herzog Encyclopedia of Religious Knowledge (Grand Rapids: Baker Book House, 1949), 13 volumes.

Smith, William, *Smith's Bible Dictionary* (rev. ed.; Grand Rapids: Zondervan Publishing House, 1953).

CHAPTER XVI

THE PHILOSOPHICAL METHOD

Etymologically considered, philosophy means "love of wisdom"; but it may be more broadly defined as reasoning or speculation concerning the problems of life, chiefly on the basis of man's wisdom and apart from the revelation of God. Basically philosophy is man's effort to solve the problems of the universe by means of human reason and as such is the direct opposite of theology, which is God's revelation concerning Himself and matters relating to man. The question may rightly be raised, then, whether or not there is any place for this method in the Christian system. The answer lies very definitely in the affirmative, for philosophy deals with the fundamental issues of life; and the Bible student will do well to discover and organize what the Bible has to say in regard to these matters. The philosophical method of Bible study, therefore, does not argue the issues but seeks to learn what God has already said about them.

Of course the field of philosophy is too vast to permit complete discussion of it in a single chapter if one is to consider separately the areas of ethics, theism, history of philosophy, political philosophy, philosophy of religion, logic, and other such subjects. It does seem possible, however, to accomplish this feat if we cut across the whole discipline of philosophy and define and discuss the six fundamental problems discernible in the field: theological, metaphysical, epistemological, ethical, political, and historical; and the present study is organized in that fashion.[1]

[1] For this arrangement the writer is primarily indebted to Castell, *An Introduction to Modern Philosophy* (New York: The Macmillan Co., 1946).

Theological problem. Succinctly stated, the theological problem is, Can a man in nature find reasons for justifying a belief in the existence of God? Logically there are only three positions that can be taken in answer to this question: (1) the skeptical approach as represented by David Hume; (2) the limited deity of John Stuart Mill; (3) the omnipotent, omniscient, omnipresent God of the Bible, as argued by Thomas Aquinas. The latter used five arguments to support his contention that nature does reveal the infinite God of faith. In the first of these he sought to demonstrate that one can argue from the change everywhere evident back to an unchanging being, the author of all change; in the second he tried to get back of the endless chain of causation to the first cause; in the third he called attention to the fact that in our experience everything seems to be contingent upon something else, and he endeavored to argue back to that which is not contingent on anything; in the fourth he proceeded from imperfection to the perfect one; and in the last from design in the universe to the wise designer.[2]

Some evangelical writers put a good deal of confidence in these arguments; others question their validity. The writer stands with the former group. As already stated in this chapter, no effort is made here to develop a philosophical apologetic or engage in prolonged discussion of any of these philosophical questions; rather, the main interest is in getting the student to collect and organize Biblical teaching relating to them. The advanced student may wish to pursue the theological problem by documenting the arguments set forth by Thomas Aquinas. He could readily point to such passages as Psalm 19:1: "The heavens declare the glory of God; and the firmament sheweth his handiwork," in dealing with the argument from design; or Malachi 3:6, "For I, Jehovah, change not; therefore ye, O sons of Jacob, are not consumed," in demonstrating the unchanging character of God in contradistinction to the change everywhere apparent in the universe. Others

---

[2] A good treatment of the theistic arguments may be found in James Orr's *The Christian View of God and the World,* now reprinted by Eerdman's Publishing Co., Grand Rapids, Michigan.

may simply wish to correlate all that the Bible states or intimates concerning the existence and nature of God.

In developing the latter, one could gain great help by looking under the general heading of "God" in such works as R. A. Torrey's *The New Topical Text Book*, H. E. Monser's *Cross Reference Digest of Bible References*, or Orville J. Nave's *Topical Bible*. By way of further example, the argument from design might be confirmed by using these same helps to see what Scripture has to say about such terms related to nature as "heavens," "earth," "sun," "moon," and "stars."

Metaphysical problem. Metaphysics is an inquiry into the question of ultimate reality, or being, or what things are made of. Some philosophers may be classified as monists — reality is found in one substance; others as dualists — all things are made of two elements; and yet others as pluralists — ultimate reality consists of several elements. Some philosophers are extremely materialistic, making even mind a product of matter; others find a place for God in their systems. A position that seems to be in line with Scriptural teaching is that God is the Eternal, a spirit being, the creator of the spirit and material worlds and that in the material world there is a pluralism of elements. In the spiritual realm are found angels — fallen and unfallen — and the non-material part of man's nature. Some argue that the non-material part of man's nature is to be classified into soul and spirit, while others do not make such a distinction. Biblical metaphysics is an intriguing study, and the student will find it interesting and profitable to locate references that substantiate and elucidate the Scriptural position described above. In this respect, the student is again encouraged to consult the topical guides mentioned in the discussion of the theological problem. Verses listed under such headings as "angels," "Satan," "spirit," "creation," and "God" will serve to elucidate the Biblical teachings on metaphysics.

Epistemological problem. Epistemology is the inquiry into the nature of knowledge. Tremendous literary efforts have been made by the philosophers to answer such questions as how we can know, if we can know, and what we can know. Generally speaking, non-Christian philosophy rests the whole basis of its discussion on empiricism — knowledge comes from experience gained by means of the five senses, and revelation has no relationship to the question. Of course, there are those such as David Hume who engage in epistemological skepticism and doubt whether man can really know anything and cast doubt even on the reality of mind or self, but most philosophers hold to some kind of demonstrable knowledge.

Distinction is made by philosophers between *a posteriori* knowledge — which is known on the basis of experience — and *a priori* — that which can be known in advance of experience; but this does not violate the assertion that non-Christian philosophy is essentially empirical, because something known *a priori* is usually held to be true on the basis of previous experience in that realm of activity. For example, one may say *a priori,* "I do not know whether there are five rooms on the first floor of that house and four on the second; but if there are, they will add up to nine." Certainly previous experience determines mathematical accuracy in this case.

Another question which arises in this field is whether we know *phenomena* (specific objects or things) or *noumena* (universals). Kant averred that we could know or experience only phenomena; we cannot experience phenomena carried out to such a degree that they become universals. Kant was right in believing that we cannot know the noumenal through reason, but we can by faith; and the greatest fact that we must accept in this way is that God has revealed Himself and we can therefore know ultimates based on that revelation. The extreme materialistic position in epistemology is that all that cannot be learned or proved by laws used in the physical sciences is not knowledge; August Comte is a representative of this school of thought.

The Biblical teaching on the subject of epistemology is that all sure knowledge is revealed; experience is of value but it is not a completely safe guide because it is easy to misjudge knowledge gained in that way — it must be purified by revelation. It is suggested that for the study of this problem the Scriptural statements on knowledge, faith, belief, and wisdom and its origin be collected and developed in such a way as to answer the principal questions raised in the field of epistemology. These and related terms which may occur to the reader as he studies Biblical epistemology, can quickly be traced through Scripture by means of a concordance. After the spade work is complete, it will be discovered that the material gathered can readily be grouped under such headings as "the source of knowledge," "the purpose of knowledge," and "the nature of knowledge."

Ethical problem. The ethical problem relates to the discovery of the principles by which we distinguish between what is right or wrong. A Christian moralist may say that ethics is the science which teaches men their duty and the reasons why this duty is encumbent upon them; right is that which is consistent with the will of God and is commanded by Him. The ethical question as usually considered even by Christians is, What is best for man? But a true Biblical ethic asks, What is best for God and brings the greatest glory to Him? That which is right measures up not primarily to His law but His nature, and that which is wrong is contrary to His nature. Non-Christian moralists determine that a course of action is right because reason prescribes it (Kant); it pays in the long run or helps the most people (Mill); it is in line with conscience; or might makes right (Nietzsche). To them, the standard for all ethical conduct is found in man or society and is therefore relativistic. The Christian, on the other hand, holds that there is no clearly defined or complete standard of conduct within man, so he must be guided from without — by God — and his ethic will therefore be absolute. It is recommended that the Bible student who is interested in a study project on this problem trace through the Scripture to discover the nature of God in order that he might have a guide for the ethical development of his personal life, for Jesus said, "Ye therefore shall be perfect, as your heavenly Father is perfect" (Matt. 5: 48).

In this connection, one might investigate the occurrences of such terms as "perfection" and "holy" or "holiness" by means of a concordance, to learn more of this attribute of God and to see how He imparts a certain amount of holiness to us or how He demands a life of holiness from us. A study of the concept of good would also provide a profitable consideration of the ethical problem. Again with the help of a concordance, look up the words "good" and "goodness." When finished, find answers to the following questions in the verses you have located: Why are certain men called good in Scripture? How is one enabled to be good? What is the result or outworking of good in the individual life? A similar process might well be followed with the concept of evil or bad. Yet another helpful study of this type could pursue the lines of a practical and devotional study of the Ten Commandments in order to develop a standard for a personal ethic.

Historical problem. Basically the historical problem is this: What is the pattern which holds the events of history together? Some believe there is no pattern; others feel that we cannot know whether or not there is a pattern; and still others say that there is a pattern. Among the latter, three basic philosophies of history are taught: the pessimistic, the optimistic, and the pessimistic-optimistic. The first of these (set forth by such men as Oswald Spengler in his *Decline of the West*) is that the world is on a downhill road to oblivion and that ultimately even the earth will stand still in its orbit and the sun will grow cold. In other words, history has no goal; it is not advancing to a purposive end.

The optimistic philosophies are generally evolutionary in approach and teach that man is getting better and/or coming to a better day. One of the most widely promulgated philosophies of this school is the Marxian view, which holds that after the revolution and dictatorship of the proletariat, there will one day emerge a new order in which there will be a classless society. The pessimistic-Optimistic position is well represented by Augustine (*City of God*) and is widely held by Christians today. This school is pessimistic in that it does not believe man can improve himself; it is optimistic in its tenet that God will one day rectify society and bring it to the utopian condition that men have always longed for. It should be of great value to the reader, if he is interested in further study on this problem, to collect and organize Scriptural teaching on God's workings in history and His prophecies as to its final outcome. Since it is difficult to suggest specific headings under which the student might find material relating to this problem, he is referred to the following references for instruction on the subject: Psalm 66:7; Daniel 2:21; 4:25, 35; Acts 17:26 (ASV); Romans 13:1; Deuteronomy 28:1, 2, 20-22, 24, 25; I Kings 11:9-13; Isaiah 11 and 35; Matthew 24, 25; Revelation 19-22. This list can be greatly expanded through the agency of such reference Bibles as the *Thompson Chain Reference Bible* and the *Scofield Reference Bible*. Helpful books bearing on this theme include *The Millennium* by W. E. Blackstone, *The Kingdom in History and Prophecy* and *Systematic Theology*, Volume IV, by L. S. Chafer, *Hath God Cast Away His People?* by A. C. Gaebelein, *Lectures on the Second Coming and Kingdom of the Lord and Savior Jesus Christ* by William Kelly, and *The Basis of Premillennial Faith* by C. C. Ryrie.

Political problem. The political problem is the justification of the state to possess sovereign power over the wills of its subjects. For many centuries it has been common for kings to claim that their power rests in divine appointment. Philosophers have had many varying views of the subject. Some held that sovereignty lay only with the people; others that it rested with a representative body chosen by the people; and still others that it is justified by the need of human nature to be restrained and coerced. The Biblical position, however, demonstrates that ultimate sovereignty inheres in God who ordains powers according to His will and for His glory and that both these powers and the people as a whole are responsible to Him. If the student is interested in pursuing this matter further, he should investigate what Scripture says about the origins and nature of authority in government, the responsibility of people to the government and government to the people, and the relations of government and God. To illustrate how such a study may be developed, two outlines worked out by students of the writer are produced here. In giving instructions for this assignment the teacher suggested that after the students completed this investigation, they would probably discover that their findings fitted generally into the categories listed above. In order to reach such a conclusion, they were encouraged to trace such words as "govern," "government," "rule," "tribute," "authority," "sovereignty," and "judge" through Scripture by means of a concordance and to note particularly instructions on relations between government and the people in Ephesians, Colossians, and Daniel.

I. Origination of Governmental Authority — God
   A. Governments are ordained of God — Romans 13:1
   B. Governmental rulers are God's ministers — Romans 13:4, 6
   C. God sets up governments and takes them down according to His own sovereign will — Daniel 4:32; 5:21; Psalm 75:7

II. Responsibilities of Government to the People
   A. The ruler is to be discreet and wise — Genesis 41:33; Deuteronomy 1:13
   B. The ruler is to minister for good and protection and is to help the poor and needy — Romans 12:4; Psalm 82:3, 4
   C. He is to recognize God, the Almighty — Psalm 2:10, 11
     1. Nebuchadnezzar — Daniel 4
     2. Belshazzar — Daniel 5

III. Responsibilities of People to the Government
   A. Rulers are not to be resisted because in doing so one resists God — Romans 13:2
     1. People are to submit to ordinances of men for the Lord's sake — I Peter 2:13, 14
     2. Despising government is a sin of the flesh (II Peter 2:10, "despise dominion," ASV)
   B. People to pay tribute to government — Romans 13:6, 7; Matthew 17:25-27
   C. Commands of rulers not obeyed when directly opposed to God's commands or God's purposes
     1. The midwives did not obey Pharaoh's orders to kill the Hebrew male babies — Exodus 1:17
     2. The Hebrew children would not worship the image

of Nebuchadnezzar — Daniel 3:18

3. Peter preached despite the orders not to do so saying, "We ought to obey God rather than men" — Acts 5:29   — *David Winget*

I. The Origin of the Authority of Government
  A. God is sovereign over human government — Psalm 75: 7; Psalm 67:4; Daniel 4:32; Romans 13:1
    1. He allows the righteous to maintain authority — II Kings 19:20-22, 34
    2. He brings judgment on those who exalt themselves above Him
      a. Nebuchadnezzar — Daniel 4:30-32
      b. Herod — Acts 12:21-23
    3. He will use an ungodly nation as a means of chastisement on a formerly righteous nation — I Kings 14:15, 16; Daniel 1:1, 2
    4. He may set up a man who is obedient to Him in place of one who has disobeyed Him — I Kings 11: 11
    5. He may take a whole family away from a place of authority because of its ungodly manner — I Kings 14:7-11
    6. Because of one man's righteousness He may allow him to maintain an heir or descendent on the throne — I Kings 11:13; Luke 1:32
  B. God will allow the people some freedom in their choice of the type of government — I Samuel 8:4-9
II. Nature of This Authority
  A. As opposed to the will of God:
    1. A ruler may use authority in an unrighteous manner to fulfill selfish desires — I Kings 21:7-14
    2. In such cases God brings judgment upon the ruler or rulers — I Kings 21:19
  B. As God has willed it:
    1. To maintain and promote the good of the people — Romans 13:3, 4
    2. To judge the evil — Romans 13:3, 4

III. Responsibility between Government and People
  A. Government:
    1. Must not lead the people to sin — I Kings 12:28-30; 13:1-3
    2. Must promote the good of the people — Romans 13: 3, 4
    3. Must judge evil — Romans 13:3, 4
    4. Must maintain internal peace — I Samuel 30:21-24
    5. Must protect the rights of its citizens — Acts 22: 25-29
  B. People:
    1. Must obey the laws — Romans 13:2, 6, 7; Mark 12:17
    2. Must serve the government — Romans 13:1
    3. Must not, however, obey human government to the extent of disobeying God — Daniel 3:16-18, 28; 6: 10, 16, 23; Mark 12:17
    4. Must pray for rulers — I Timothy 2:1, 2
                                        —*Charles Ford*

In the Middle Ages, philosophy was the handmaiden of theology. Such great thinkers as Anselm took as their basic approach: "I believe in order to understand." That is to say, faith must precede understanding; but it must not be felt that in his system faith excluded all efforts to understand by means of philosophical investigation. In a day when philosophy has been so thoroughly divorced from theology and has been used to attack the fundamentals of the faith, we need to return to the position of Anselm and develop a new Christian philosophy based on revelation. If philosophy is the endeavor to solve the problems of the universe and everyday life, then let us turn to the Book of Books to discover there the answers to the difficulties and perplexities of our time as God has propounded them.

BIBLIOGRAPHY

Listed below are a few of the better introductions to philosophy. No attempt is made to provide a bibliography for the entire field. Special attention is called to the new works by J. M. Spier and Warren Young.

Beck, Lewis, *Philosophic Inquiry, An Introduction to Philosophy* (New York: Prentice-Hall, Inc., 1953).

Castell, Alburey, *An Introduction to Modern Philosophy* (New York: The Macmillan Co., 1946).

Hocking, William Ernest, *Types of Philosophy* (New York: Charles Scribner's Sons, 1939).

McCormick, John F., *Scholastic Metaphysics* (Chicago: Loyola University Press, 1940).

Patrick, George T. W., *Introduction to Philosophy* (New York: Houghton Mifflin, 1935).

Bandall, John H., and Justus Buchler, *Philosophy: An Introduction* (New York: Barnes & Noble, 1942).

Spier, J. M., *An Introduction to Christian Philosophy* (Philadelphia: Presbyterian and Reformed Publishing Co., 1954).

Titus, Harold H., *Living Issues in Philosophy* (New York: American Book Co., 1946).

Young, Warren, *A Christian Approach to Philosophy* (Wheaton, Illinois: Van Kampen Press, 1954).

CHAPTER XVII

THE PSYCHOLOGICAL METHOD

If one were to consult a dictionary for a definition of psychology, he might find something like the following: a science which treats of the mind, the phenomena of consciousness and behavior, traits, feelings, actions and attributes of the human personality as an individual and in society. This phraseology could well be abbreviated to state that psychology is a study of human behavior. It should be said, however, that psychologists do not now seem to be as concerned with stating what psychology is as they are with what it seeks to do; in that vein Munn says, "Today the psychologist sees his task as describing and discovering the environmental and biological bases of conduct. His ultimate aim is to further our understanding of ourselves and our fellows so that we can better predict and control the course of human events."[1] Taking the same general approach, Ruch may be quoted as follows: "Broadly considered, psychology seeks to understand the abilities, motives, thinking, and doing of people and is closely related to biology, anthropology, and sociology."[2]

Psychology is a vast field, whole majors being devoted to it in a large majority of American colleges and universities; it will be necessary therefore to limit the discussion here to a brief mention of those aspects of the field which seem to relate most clearly to this type of Scriptural investigation. Five topics are considered.

[1] Norman L. Munn, *Psychology: Fundamentals of Human Adjustment* (2nd edition; New York: Houghton Mifflin Co., 1951), pp. 1, 2.
[2] Floyd L. Ruch, *Psychology and Life* (4th edition; Chicago: Scott, Foresman and Co., 1953), p. 6.

Heredity and environment. Technical discussion of chromosomes, genes, and other factors involved in human reproduction is quite beyond the scope of this study, but it should be obvious to all that inherited characteristics of temperament and physique do affect one's relationships with others. Details of such subjects may be learned from some of the excellent works on psychology listed at the end of this chapter. Not only do hereditary features condition human relations, but so does the environment in which the human organism is socialized; the importance of environment must not be pushed too far, however. The non-Christian psychologist usually evaluates man on the horizontal plane only. That is to say, he is to be observed for what he is and for the way he reacts to an environment, without the intervention of an outside force that might be called God. By many, personality is considered to be the end product of the environment of physical nature combined with the ideas and established practices of men in association with each other. The Christian psychologist, however, may be described as three dimensional in his view of man because he considers the nature of the organism, his environment, *and God.*

That one's social context does influence his attitudes and actions greatly is universally agreed upon, but all factors do not influence everyone in the same way; nor is it always possible to determine the environmental factors that account for the actions of a given person. Since environment matters so much, it is important for us to do our utmost to insure the best possible surroundings for ourselves and for those for whom we are responsible. Perhaps one of the greatest blessings that can come to a Christian in a study of this kind is the realization that he is not completely at the mercy of his environment but can overcome it. Of course, the non-Christian speaks much of surmounting obstacles, but he is limited to his own resources; we have at our disposal all the resources of divine omnipotence.

Personality and adjustment. "Personality is the sum total of everything that constitutes a person's mental, emotional, and temperamental make-up."[3] Psychologists attempt to deal with

---

[3] Joseph Tiffin, *et. al., The Psychology of Normal People* (rev. edition; Boston: D. C. Heath and Co., 1946), p. 100.

the human personality by observing its actions and reactions and suggesting means by which such activity may be improved. Sometimes they recommend a better environment, sometimes more education, and at other times a new type of approach to the problems of life — but all of this is apart from the Christian interpretation of the human organism. They do not recognize the fall of Adam and his federal headship of the human race, the Biblical claim that the whole world now is under the dominion of Satan, nor that social problems and conflicts arise because of the presence of sin in the world. Therefore, they fail to understand that many of the problems of the individual will be solved when the sin problem is properly treated.

Whether the personality be interpreted from the standpoint of the secular or Christian psychologist, the problem of adjustment still remains. It is the plague of humanity that it constantly faces difficulties and frustration. The former can usually be overcome; when they become more or less insurmountable, they fall into the frustration category. The source of frustration may be environmental, personal, or internal conflict.

In the first grouping come such items as the continued barking of a dog when we are trying to sleep, legal restrictions, or economic difficulties; in the second, physical deformity or blemishes, inferiority complex over some real or imagined shortcoming, and the like; in the third, frustration arises when an individual has two strong but opposing motives and must choose which one to satisfy at the expense of the other.

When frustrations are severe or improperly handled, they can produce unhealthy patterns of adjustive behavior or can even cause severe mental disorders. If there has been unsatisfactory adjustment of the individual and his surroundings, any of a number of inadequate reactions might occur: bragging, teasing and cruelty, timidity, show of temper, jealousy, lying, and stealing. In addition to these, frustration often leads one to give vent to certain compensatory mechanisms which permit activity in another direction in order to make up for the loss or difficulty sustained in the situation originally engaged in. Sometimes the individual utilizes an escape mechanism such as a flight from reality or a flight into reality — losing one's self in a round of activity. At other times he may belittle or blame others for his own failures. Again, he may engage in rationalization — persuading one's self that an act was all right even though it may not have been. Occasionally a person will find release in regression — engaging in such childish acts as weeping or stamping the feet; or in aggression — a show of temper or cruelty. Repression is yet another compensation; in this case one refuses to admit the existence of difficulties. Lastly, it is not uncommon for people to capitalize a defect in order to gain sympathy and escape the ordinary responsibilities of life.

Feelings and emotions. Feelings are a mild type of emotion, and emotion may be defined as "an experience involving a disturbed condition of the organism brought about by the prospect of some value's being gained or lost, and involving also an impulse to act."[4] Emotions are caused or affected by psychological conditions within the body, the accumulation of human experience over a period of time, and external situations that the individual may meet moment by moment. The emotional element in man's nature is not to be deprecated; it is absolutely necessary to his physical survival. Emotions stimulate the body to action in the face of danger; they give rise to greater activity at the mental level; they liberate one from the effects of certain inhibitions; and they provide the variety and color which are so necessary to life (what would life be like without joy or love or the ability to sympathize with a friend?).

Unsatisfactory emotional adjustment will definitely prove to be a handicap to the individual who wishes to lead a normal, happy life. Expressions of anger, jealousy, and worry may mutilate skill, alienate friends, and prove detrimental to mental and physical health. It is desirable, therefore, that the individual overcome such activity and arrive at an emotional maturity, which one may be said to have attained in its fullest sense when he has learned to control his emotions and at the same time possess a high degree of inner peace and harmony. In other words, such maturity is not merely repressionism; it is the change of the inner life. Of course, the efforts of the psy-

4 *Ibid.,* p. 263.

chologist alone cannot accomplish this goal; there must be the special ministration of the Holy Spirit.

There are, however, a few common sense observations that may be made on this general subject: (1) Avoid situations that are known to produce excessive emotion. (2) Develop an ideal of control. The person who prides himself on acting as he feels, who thinks it a weakness to keep everything under cover, stands a poor chance of reaching emotional maturity. (3) Understand the nature of emotions and view them objectively. (4) Achieve understanding and mastery of the situation. Fear, anger, and worry often disappear when we see a situation in its true light. (5) Prevent the overt expression of the emotion. Be thrifty rather than spendthrift in the expression of emotion.[5]

Lest the reader be led to feel that this discussion has advocated an old-fashioned repressionism, a word of caution should be given here. Truth does not lie in extremes: an excessive form of repressionism can warp the personality; on the other hand, a completely free expressionism would wreck society. A happy medium must be found wherein the individual can develop happily and freely and yet avoid harm or offense to his fellow man.

Motivation of behavior. Psychologists are not agreed on their use of such terms as *motive, drive,* and *instinct;* neither do they all concur on which of these urges in man are innate and which are socially learned. General unanimity does seem to exist, however, in respect to the fact that basic physiological drives of hunger, thirst, and sex, and the satisfaction of basic requirements of air, heat, and cold are innate. When such drives as fear are considered, there is quite a divergence of opinion. Some hold that one is born with a fear instinct — a relatively complicated unlearned pattern of reflexes — and they try to demonstrate that this is true by pointing out the sounds and situations from which a baby shrinks. Others say that fear is acquired and use as proof that the child who is never taught to fear snakes will come to maturity without developing a strong aversion to them. It is not the purpose of the present

[5] *Ibid.,* pp. 306, 307.

study to debate the question of whether certain urges are inherited or acquired; it is rather the plan to point out that they do exist in the normal personality and to show that they must be reckoned with in the psychological method of Bible study.

In addition to the physiological drives listed above, there are a number of others to which attention should be drawn. Bogardus feels that the four fundamental drives are the urge for new experience, for security, for response, and for recognition.[6] Monroe agrees in part but injects other elements in his listing of the four basic urges: self-preservation and the desire for physical well-being, freedom from external restraint, preservation and increase of self-esteem, and preservation of the human race.[7] Other drives or urges which lead men to act as they do include acquisition and saving, creating, curiosity, destruction, competition, imitation, loyalty, personal enjoyment, power and authority, pride, reverence or worship, revulsion, and sympathy. These drives are common to all, and the successful advertiser or teacher must reckon with them; the Christian worker will seek to sublimate them in the service of the Lord.

Mental health. A person may be said to possess a certain degree of mental health if he has relative control of his emotions and desires and a fair amount of ability to meet frustrating experiences. Admittedly, the mental health of the American people has been on the decline in recent years; and with the rising number of abnormal individuals seeking admission to our hospitals has come increased concern for the study, prevention, and cure of abnormality. Coleman feels that faulty parent-child relations, trauma, frustration, and conflict are among the major psychological factors in the development of psychoses.[8] The first cause listed is certainly in line with the greater divorce rate and apparent disintegration of the American home. Trauma, which may be defined as shock or injury, is always a by-product of war.

[6] Emory S. Bogardus, *Sociology* (3rd ed., New York: Macmillan, 1950), pp. 76, 77.
[7] Alan H. Monroe, *Principles and Types of Speech* (3rd ed., Chicago: Scott, Foresman and Co.,), p. 194.
[8] James C. Coleman, *Abnormal Psychology and Modern Life* (Chicago: Scott, Foresman and Co., 1950), p 234.

The treatment of mental cases is primarily a medical or psychiatric question of such magnitude and technicality that discussion here is impossible. It may be said, however, that a virile Christian experience is one of the greatest deterrents to mental disorder; though the Christian faith should not be considered as a cure-all and certainly does not displace medical attention of mental cases.

Psychotic disorders are divided into two general groups: functional and organic psychoses. The latter are caused by such factors as head injuries, epilepsy, degenerative diseases of the nervous system, and the like. The former relate more particularly to frustrations and maladjustments of one type or another. A number of the functional psychoses need to be listed and defined. While the writer is familiar with some of the classifications of these psychoses, he does not deem it necessary to this study to develop that line of thought.

1. *Mania.* A mania is a violent desire or passion that possesses an individual. Several forms are based on this root: pyromania — a passion for fire; dipsomania — an uncontrollable compulsion to drink; megalomania — a fancy that one is some great or wealthy person; monomania — unbalance on one subject; kleptomania — a compulsion to steal.

2. A *hypochondriac* is a person who continually complains about imaginary ills.

3. The *manic-depressive* state is characterized by extreme ups and downs of mood. Delusions and hallucinations are often present; vile language and curses are common. Sometimes this type needs to be kept under restraint.

4. The *schizophrenic* is a split or divided personality that loses contact with his environment and lives in an unreal world of his own.

5. A *melancholiac* lives in a fixed state of dejection.

6. A *paranoiac* has delusions of persecution.

In utilizing the psychological method, the student seeks to look at a portion of Scripture through the eyes of the psychologist, evaluating the individuals he meets there in the light of this science and interpreting the events from the standpoint of its terminology and outlook. He will find the brief outline provided in this chapter to be a helpful guide for his study, and the example will demonstrate in part how he may proceed with projects of his own choosing.

DEVELOPMENT OF EXAMPLE

By way of example of the possibilities of this method, a brief treatment of the relations of David and Saul is detailed here. To begin with, it may be observed that David possessed a relatively high degree of mental health, which seems to stem from the fact that he had an abiding faith in God that carried him through most of the vicissitudes of life. Saul, on the other hand, developed into what may be termed a manic-depressive. In this respect, we should note first of all the Biblical statement that an evil spirit came upon him (I Sam. 16:14; 19:9); and secondly, he passed through alternating moods of depression, rage, and normalcy. Seemingly this mental condition was brought on by a frustration derangement: God was against him; Jonathan had lined up with David in opposition to him; he lived under the realization that his days were numbered; and he suffered greatly from hurt pride. To all of this his personality was unable to make adjustment; the one person who might have saved Saul in his hour of need was God, but He had placed His servant under judgment for disobedience. Some of Saul's personality maladjustments were bragging (I Sam. 15:13); jealousy (18:8); temper tantrums (20:30, 31); cruelty (18:11; 22:17-19); and rationalization (23:7).

In all of the struggle between the two leaders, David faced many frustrating experiences; but he demonstrated again and again that man is not completely conditioned by his circumstances. More than once the whole cause seemed lost, but he continued doggedly on; more than once he had occasion to take the life of his enemy, but he determined not to do so — divine love and wisdom led him to avoid taking Saul's life. On two occasions, however, David's difficulties were too much for him, and in frustration he sought refuge among the enemies of Israel. The first of these occurrences took place soon after his flight from the court of Saul. At that time it seemed that the place of refuge which he could reach most quickly was the court of

Achish, king of Gath. When he arrived there, the king called attention to the Hebrew warrior's victories over the Philistines, and David in fear feigned madness (I Sam. 21). The second occasion of David's flight to Gath came after he had been pursued by Saul for an extended period of time, and his will to resist was worn down. As is so often true, physical strain reduces mental and spiritual resistance; and David experienced a lapse of faith (I Sam. 27).

In conclusion, it is interesting to observe the way in which several urges or drives influenced the actions of the two principals of this narrative. As already mentioned, Monroe lists the urge to self-preservation and the desire for physical well-being among the basic urges. Both David and Saul were driven by this motive to rather extreme measures. When fleeing from the court of Saul, David lied to Ahimelech, the priest, in order to secure food and a sword (I Sam. 21). Shortly thereafter, he feigned madness in the court of Achish, the king of Gath, in order to preserve himself from assassination at the hands of his enemies. At a later time, when he felt he could no longer hold out against the pursuits of Saul, David fled again to the court of Achish; this time he lied to Achish about his invasion of the territory to the south of Ziglag because he feared that if the king learned of his exploits, he might drive David into Judean territory once more, and he would again have to run from Saul. Saul, on the other hand, wanted to preserve his kingdom from David and sought on two occasions to kill him (I Sam. 20:31; 24:20-22). Unsuccessful in this and deprived of the sage counsel of Samuel, Saul was driven to other extremes of conduct and even resorted to a mistress of a divining demon (see Hebrew of I Sam. 28:7) at Endor. It may be observed further concerning this drive that Saul appealed to the acquisitive or self-preservation instinct of the Israelites when he made the following statement in a speech soliciting popular support against David: "Hear now, ye Benjamites; will the son of Jesse give every one of you fields and vineyards, will he make you all captains of thousands and captains of hundreds" (I Sam. 22:7).

Preservation and the increase of self-esteem is another basic urge that shows up in the actions of Saul. He was head and shoulders taller than any other Jew (I Sam. 9:20), and his father was a mighty man (9:1). Saul defeated the Ammonites (11:11), and he had further victories. Then David came into the picture. Saul was big and brave, but David had his victory too — killing Goliath and his ten thousands, while Saul only killed his thousands; also the Spirit was on David. Naturally, Saul reacted in an effort to preserve his self-esteem and became suspicious of David. Suspicion and envy led to grosser sins and the gap between them became too wide to bridge.

Related to these basic urges are three others that are exemplified in the narrative of I Samuel. The first is fear, which is demonstrated on the part of Saul, who was afraid of David because the Lord was with him (18:2, 29), and he responded in many ways already described. David, on the other hand, was afraid of Saul's task force that constantly dogged his steps; he ran from Saul, lied, and feigned madness (21 and 27).

Another drive that may be noted in the David-Saul conflict is pride; this is responsible for God's rejection of Saul prior to his mentally deranged condition. Saul's pride led to his usurpation of the priest's office and offering of sacrifice (I Sam. 13) and his incomplete obedience (15). Last, sympathy comes into the account as Saul tries to stir up support for his cause. In this vein, he whimpers: "all of you have conspired against me, and there is none that discloseth to me when my son maketh a league with the son of Jesse, and there is none of you that is sorry for me, or discloseth unto me that my son hath stirred up my servant against me, to lie in wait, as at this day?" (22:8).

The psychological method of Bible study may be utilized for all types of Biblical characters; it should not be limited to the abnormal personalities. Of special interest in any such development will be the question of why the individual acted as he did or the motivation involved in his activity. Probably the believer will pay particular attention to the spiritual condition of the person under consideration and the effects of that condition on his general actions; for any Christian approach to psychology is conditioned by the fact that man possesses a fallen nature which is in conflict with divine principles, and the degree to which that nature is controlled by the Holy Spirit determines the direction of the thoughts and deeds of the individual.

SUGGESTIONS FOR FURTHER STUDY

The value of the use of this method for effective Bible study may be demonstrated further by the enumeration of a few suggestions for further study.

1. An evaluation of motives for Christian service in Philippians 1:14-19 and Paul's reaction to them.

2. The influence of Solomon's environment on his policies and practices.

3. A study of the way in which Paul's Christian experience affected his reactions to the vicissitudes suffered during his ministry.

4. A tabulation of the human emotions and feelings of Christ as noted in the Gospels, with a brief mention of the circumstances prompting each.

5. A psychological investigation of the actions toward or reactions to Jesus on the part of the Pharisees.

6. A psychological treatment of the actions and attitudes of Elijah after the Mount Carmel incident.

7. A psychological interpretation of the Book of Jonah.

8. A psychological study of the motives for the methods of opposition to Nehemiah.

9. An evaluation of the emotions expressed at the laying of the foundations of the second temple (Ezra 3).

10. The psychological factors involved in the institution of Jeroboam's false worship.

BIBLIOGRAPHY

Allport, Gordon W., *Personality—A Psychological Interpretation* (New York: Henry Holt & Co., 1937).

Coe, George A., *The Motives of Men* (New York: Charles Scribner's Sons, 1928).

Coleman, James C., *Abnormal Psychology and Modern Life* (Chicago: Scott, Foresman and Co., 1950).

Cross, Hildreth, *An Introduction to Psychology* (Grand Rapids: Zondervan Publishing House, 1952). Conservative Christian approach.

Emerson, Wallace, *Outline of Psychology* (Wheaton, Illinois: Van Kampen Press, 1953). Conservative Christian approach.

English, O. S., and G. H. J. Pearson, *Emotional Problems of Living* (New York: W. W. Norton & Co., Inc., 1945).

Guthrie, Edwin R., *The Psychology of Human Conflict* (New York: Harper & Brothers, 1938).

Ligon, Ernest, *The Psychology of Christian Personality* (New York: Macmillan & Co., 1950).

Merton, Robert, *Mass Persuasion* (New York: Harper & Brothers, 1946).

Munn, Norman L., *Psychology: Fundamentals of Human Adjustment* (2nd edition; New York: Houghton Mifflin Co., 1951).

Ruch, Floyd L., *Psychology and Life* (4th edition; Chicago: Scott Foresman and Co., 1953).

Tiffin, Joseph, Frederic B. Knight, and Eston J. Asher, *The Psychology of Normal People* (rev. edition; Boston: D. C. Heath & Co., 1946).

CHAPTER XVIII

THE DEVOTIONAL METHOD

"Devotional study is not so much a technique as a spirit. It is the spirit of eagerness which seeks the mind of God; it is the spirit of humility which listens readily to the voice of God; it is the spirit of adventure which pursues earnestly the will of God; it is the spirit of adoration which rests in the presence of God."[1] While it is true that the spirit with which one approaches Bible study is of prime importance, method also looms large as its basis and in its procedure. The methods detailed in the foregoing chapters should often be of value in furnishing a means of understanding Scripture in order that a true devotional application may be made; moreover, devotionalizing takes on more significance and makes a greater impact when developed in accordance with a plan.

Before speaking specifically concerning ways of organizing devotional study, however, a few preliminary remarks might be in order. First of all, it is in the pursuance of this method that Satan will raise his greatest opposition. He may not be too concerned when the believer endeavors to study the Bible from the scientific, philosophical, or psychological standpoint; but when he starts to apply the Word to his personal life in order to have a more victorious life and thereby to present a more effective witness, the story is quite different. The Evil One will do all in his power to prevent such an eventuality, and the believer will soon discover increasing temptation coming his way to spend his time on things other

[1] M. C. Tenney, *Galatians: The Charter of Christian Liberty*, pp. 189-90.

than personal Bible study. Second, the Bible student should avoid in his devotional life overemphasis on either intensive or extensive consideration of Scripture; the two go together. Too much time spent on intensive investigation causes a loss of an appreciation of the over-all picture; undue attention to a general survey robs one of the blessing gained by close observation. Third, the devotional enjoyment of the Word is enhanced immeasurably by Scripture memorization. If one stores numerous passages in his heart, they will be there always for meditation and correction of life; and this is the only possible way for God's blessed man to meditate day and night in the law of the Lord (Ps. 1:2). It is of great benefit to the minister, too, if he will commit his Scripture lesson to memory far in advance of his actual homiletical work on it, for in this way the truth of the passage will permeate his whole being; and his sermon will be a part of him when he comes to deliver it. Fourth, it should be observed that there is a real need for system in the devotional method; without some sort of plan, one tends to daydream or waste time or he easily becomes satisfied with snatches or tidbits of spiritual truth which are gained by a grazing process. Let us not be as sheep wandering around in the pasture of God's Word, but rather let us drink deep at the springs of spiritual blessing.

The end in view in all devotional Bible study is the improvement of the individual's spiritual life by discovering in the Word the claims of God upon the believer and His instructions for living and enhancing the Christian life. While it is true that a certain amount of spiritual profit will be gained in pursuing all of the methods detailed in this book, perhaps even greater blessings will be reaped from a deployment of several of them in a slightly different way. The devotional method may be effectively executed by means of a careful study of words, verses, paragraphs, chapters, books, Biblical characters, and Christ in a given portion.

Words. To a certain extent a devotional study of Biblical words overlaps the theological method, but here an effort is made to view terms and concepts from a spiritual stand-point rather than in a technical way; it is wise therefore to choose words that will readily convey a spiritual message. After the choice is made, several questions may be asked of the word.

1. How is it used in the Bible; what definition may be gleaned by means of a consideration of its employment in various Biblical contexts?

2. What did it mean to those who used it? For instance, when Paul said, "For I know whom I have believed, and I am persuaded that he is able to guard that which I have committed unto him against that day" (II Tim. 1:12b), what significance did he attach to his use of "know," "believed," " persuaded," and "committed"?

3. What does it reveal of God, man, sin, and evil powers?

4. How can I relate it to the strengthening of my own spiritual life?

In addition, each individual word will submit to a bevy of questions not necessarily applicable to other terms. For example, in dealing with "wisdom" we should take note of its source — God; basis of impartation — "Trust in Jehovah with all thy heart, and lean not upon thine own understanding" (Prov. 3:5); purpose of impartation — that we might walk in right paths and bear a good testimony; and need for it — minds and hearts perverted by sin.

Verses. To be sure, verse divisions are artificial and many times they embody incomplete thoughts; but many of them afford fruitful devotional meditation. Though verses are brief, their message is often perceived by outlining the text. It may also be of value to consider the verbs in a given verse — note tense, voice, mood, message, subject, and object. Then ask yourself who authored the passage and how it fits into his over-all message or vitally contributes to it. It is difficult to give an extensive plan to be utilized in the prosecution of this kind of study because each verse is usually quite different from the others and therefore demands an individual approach, so a few suggestions of verses that could be delved into with profit are

made at this point. Great three-sixteens of the New Testament
have always drawn the attention of believers; some of the more
significant are John — salvation set forth; I Timothy — the mystery revealed; II Timothy — the Word inspired; I John — supreme
sacrifices; I Corinthians — the indwelling Spirit; and James — the
evil of disunity. Great blessing may be found also in a comparison of the verses in the Gospels which record the dying
words and acts of Christ, the statements of John the Baptist
about Christ, or the reactions of individual disciples to the call
of Christ.

Paragraphs. Many suggestions have already been made about
the study of paragraphs in Chapter II, but the approach is
slightly different in developing the devotional method. We are
not primarily concerned at this point with technical aspects
but seek rather food for our souls. Often a paragraph of Scripture (as arranged in the American Standard Version) is just the
right length for a morning or evening devotional period. One
may study paragraphs consecutively through a book, or one
may prefer the selection of paragraphs according to their subject matter. For instance, meditation on individual paragraphs
dealing with the baptism, temptation, crucifixion, and ascension
of Christ or a comparison of all paragraphs on any one of these
subjects should yield great spiritual blessing. In an effort to
ascertain the message of a paragraph, the student will do well
to give it a title, outline it, find its key verse, summarize its
content, and record the specific ways in which its statements
have spoken to his heart. The latter is of prime importance in
developing this method, and the seeker should stay with the
text until at least one entry is made under that heading.

Chapters and books. A study of the Bible by chapters and
books is combined here because if the Bible is studied by chapters, chances are that the individual will choose chapters consecutively within a book until he has completed his investigation
of the book. If the reader is interested in devotional study of
an entire book without deference to chapter divisions, he may
direct his study along lines set forth in the discussion of the inductive, synthetic, or analytical methods.

The chapter method of Bible study has long been a favorite

with Christians, and whole books have been given over to this approach. One of these works that has gained great popularity is Dr. G. Campbell Morgan's *Great Chapters of the Bible,* in which forty-nine chapters are treated.

Many different approaches to this type of Bible study have been made. For instance, Miss Grace Saxe recommends that the following ten questions be used as a guide in arriving at the fullest appreciation of a chapter:

    I. What is the principal subject of this chapter?
    II. What is the leading lesson of this chapter?
    III. Which is the best verse in this chapter?
    IV. Who are the principal persons in this chapter?
    V. What does the chapter teach concerning Christ?
    VI. Is there, in this chapter, any example for me to follow?
    VII. Is there, in this chapter, any error for me to avoid?
    VIII. Is there, in this chapter, any duty for me to perform?
    IX. Is there, in this chapter, any promise for me to claim?
    X. Is there, in this chapter, any prayer for me to echo?[2]

It is the opinion of the writer, however, that one of the simplest and most effective ways to examine a chapter is through an adaptation of the Navigators' study plan. Meditation on each chapter is prefaced by prayer, slow silent reading, and reading aloud. Then verse by verse observation is made and findings are listed under several headings: chapter title, key verse, significant truth, cross references, difficulties (personal and possible), applications, and summary or outline. In developing this plan it is recommended that large-sized loose-leaf or spiral notebooks be used. Columns with the headings just listed should then be arranged on two sheets facing each other. The first four items will require much narrower columns than the others. Place the name of the book and chapter number in the left corner of the page.

Many of these headings are self-explanatory, but brief comments may clarify some of them. The column headed "significant truth" will contain the main teaching of the chapter stated in briefest possible terms; cross references are not a necessary item, but often the Holy Spirit calls to mind parallel passages

2 Wilbur M. Smith, *Profitable Bible Study*, p. 33.

when one is meditating on the Word. There will be a sub-division of the column headed "difficulties." In one half will be listed the actual problems and questions that come to mind during the course of one's study; their solution is usually postponed until a later time. In the other half of the column will appear possible difficulties; those that do not bother the reader, but which he recognizes will trouble some and concerning which he must be prepared with an explanation. Applications are the specific commands and implications of the text which speak to the heart of the believer and lead him into a richer Christian life.

Many books of the Bible will prove to be rich mines of spiritual blessing when approached from the standpoint of the chapter method; among them are John, Romans, Hebrews, and I John. Some of the great chapters that may well be studied in this way are I Kings 8, 18; II Kings 18-19; Psalms 1, 23, 119; Isaiah 53; Luke 2; John 3, 15; Acts 2; Romans 8; I Corinthians 13, 15; Philippians 2; Hebrews 11; and I John 3.

Biblical characters. The study of Biblical characters has been treated in some length in the consideration of the biographical method. Not much need be added here except to call attention to the fact that the devotional spirit ought to be emphasized. Uppermost in the mind of the reader should be the following questions: Why did God include this person in sacred Scripture? Why did He deal with him in the manner in which He did? What is there in his life that I should emulate or avoid? What in the individual's background and associations caused him to be what he was and act as he did? If Scripture were still being written, would my name be included and if so, what would be said about me?

Christ. A. M. Hodgkin has written a book entitled *Christ in All the Scriptures,* and certainly Christ is central in the message of the entire Bible. With great blessing and profit the believer could study each book to look for prophecies, types, and direct statements concerning Jesus Christ. As in so many other aspects of the devotional method, there is overlapping here with a method previously discussed — the theological method; again the difference of study is mainly one of spirit. The reader will find outlines and suggestions for studying the person of Christ in Chapter VIII.

Whatever the approach the believer chooses in his devotional study of the Bible, it is the opinion of the writer that such a development will be much more effective when finds are recorded, because divine claims on the individual life make a greater impact when they appear in ink or type than they do when they merely pass through the mind for a fleeting moment. Moreover, devotional blessings will then be preserved as a reminder to the heart of that which God has spoken in the past.

Chapter XIX

METHODS OF TEACHING THE BIBLE

Having occupied ourselves with the various methods of studying the Bible, let us now go on to consider how to teach it. The Lord does not bestow spiritual knowledge on us purely for our enjoyment any more than He endues us with spiritual power for our blessing alone. A Bible student is merely a steward who is entrusted with the truth of God, and it is expected that he will dispense it according to the direction of the Lord, to whom he is obligated and to whom he belongs. And it must be added that privilege always brings responsibility and that the greater knowledge of Scripture one possesses, the heavier is his obligation to disseminate it.

A study of this field is too tremendous in magnitude to permit complete treatment in such a brief compass; therefore it is limited to teaching on the adult level. Moreover, the aim is not to present a formal study in educational psychology but to provide a few practical observations and principles for the teacher of the Word of God.

The Teacher

There are three prime requisites for a successful Bible teacher: (1) he must know the truth; (2) he must live the truth; and (3) he must know how to proclaim the truth. It has been the purpose of the foregoing chapters to provide means whereby one may learn the truth; it is the design of the present one to demonstrate a few observations concerning the way in which he might more effectively pass on to others what he has learned;

but neither the knowledge nor the telling of the truth means much if the teacher is not an incarnate example of the principles he professes. In this regard Monroe makes the following observation: "Nearly nineteen hundred years ago Quintilian said that a good speaker must first of all be a good man: he must be intelligent and observant, but above all he must have integrity of character. The truth of this observation has been emphasized by every writer on the subject from the days of Aristotle to the present time. People do not listen merely to a speech, but to a *person speaking;* and they are influenced quite as much by their confidence in the speaker as by what he says. The man who is honest and sincere, who has a reputation for knowing the facts and speaking the truth, is respected when he speaks because people believe in his integrity. He influences his listeners by his own character — by what classical writers used to call 'ethical persuasion.' "[1] If this is true of the general public speaker, how much more should it apply to the Christian teacher, whose whole message is ethical in nature.

Three other basic requirements for the Christian instructor must be listed before proceeding further. These are equal with or transcend the preceding and are assumptions which underlie the entire scope of this work: the teacher must have faith in God and the Bible as the Word of God, and he must realize the importance and value of teaching. Without an experience of salvation, he is incapable of perceiving the truths he wishes to impart because the "natural man receiveth not the things of the Spirit of God" (I Cor. 2:14a). Without a belief in the Word of God, he is bereft of a message and will be forced to turn aside to moralizing and social welfare. Without a perception of the value and importance of his task, he is robbed of a sense of mission and the dynamic which effectively propels him toward the realization of a specific goal.

In addition to these basic requirements, there are many others that contribute to the success or failure of the teacher. Something has already been said about knowing the truth, but additional comments on the subject are in order at this point. It is

---

[1] Alan H. Monroe, *Principles and Types of Speech*, pp. 5, 6.

of great importance for the instructor to realize that he must know more than is required by a given situation; the principle is true whether teaching a Sunday-school lesson, elementary French, or ancient history. It is the natural thing for us to try to get by with the least possible preparation, but that does not make for effective teaching; such a practice will not train the student in the most thorough manner, nor will it contribute to the self-confidence of the teacher or a high interest on the part of the pupil.

The Sunday-school teacher who is dealing with a passage in Ephesians 2 will do a much better job if he knows the design of the whole book or the general doctrinal development of the New Testament; the instructor in French grammar will understand better how to guide his charges in their study if he has read Molière and other French literature in which grammatical principles are utilized and exceptions to them observed; the ancient history professor will develop a much more effective lecture on the Parthenon if he is acquainted with the techniques of Greek art and architecture. Of course, it is impossible to acquire all of this background for every given class period; one who would teach must, therefore, constantly seek to improve his knowledge of his field.

Not only should the teacher seek to know his subject; he must like it. Enthusiasm is contagious, just as the contrary is true. Everyone knows that it is extremely difficult to have enthusiasm for a subject in which he has little or no interest; in the same degree it will be hard for that instructor to instill a high degree of interest in his students. Unfortunately, the teacher does not always have a great deal to say about some of the courses which he is called upon to teach, but in many cases the situation can be remedied. Frequently, lack of interest is due to the fact that inadequate preparation over a long period of time has developed within the individual such a feeling of insecurity that he loses his desire to teach a subject. Again, poor physical condition often causes a lapse in the teacher's zest for his work; in this case, medical attention and the restoration to health usually rekindles the fire of enthusiasm. Other teachers who really are interested in their subject matter sometimes become careless in manifesting an interest in it; such action is just as detrimental to learning as the attitude of those who really have a dislike for what they are doing. It must be remembered that warm-hearted, enthusiastic teaching without great knowledge often accomplishes more than well-prepared mechanical instruction.

The good teacher must also like his pupils. He cannot treat them as automatons and expect to achieve the maximum progress; he cannot act unkindly and impatiently toward them and expect them to respond readily to the program he wishes to promulgate. Any true teacher is sincerely and deeply interested in each of his pupils as a person; but let him make sure that his demonstration of kindness is genuine because affected kindness is a sham that is soon detected, and one's ministry suffers greatly when it is found out.

Not only must the teacher like his pupils, but he should know them, for it is only in that way he will be enabled to understand their instructional needs, impediments, likes, and dislikes. Many a teacher who has never had a course in education has become a good teacher by observing and learning from his pupils. Conversely, many who have studied education widely have failed miserably in their teaching because of their failure to study their students.

Another requirement of an effective teacher is that he have a good memory. Generally speaking, one possesses a good memory not because of heritage but through cultivation and development; and in these days of emphasis on education and psychology, the person with a poor memory is not left to his own devices because plenty of books and courses are available in memory training. It may be, however, that many of us do not realize the importance of a dependable memory; a teacher without one is dangerous. Every mistake made in class for this reason — as well as for any other — is multiplied an untold number of times, and the harm done may be incalculable. In some cases, the student is merely robbed of the best understanding of a subject, as would be true if an instructor were to say that the Venerable Bede and Alfred the Great were contemporary; but at other times the result could be loss of life, especially if a chemistry teacher were to forget the correct proportions or elements for a laboratory experiment and an explosion were to occur.

A final qualification of a good teacher is that he has will power. Without it anarchy or chaos may conquer the classroom because the instructor faces the resistance of those who dislike work, the antipathy of those who rebel against authority, and the desultory actions of those who do not like to concentrate. It must be recognized, however, that while the instructor should always be in control of a classroom situation, in the last analysis he will not be able to force the student to produce academic activity; but he must have a determination to go to all ends to generate sufficient interest or desire on the part of the student so that he will eagerly engage in academic pursuits. Creativity, then, rather than control should be the primary result of will power.

Now let us pass from the positive to the negative. There are two chief errors into which teachers fall. The first is that they are frequently too academic. To some such an assertion would suggest that the vocabulary he uses is beyond the grasp of the students; to others it would imply that the material is presented in a theoretical way and has little relationship to the practical problems of daily life; to yet others it would convey the idea of a certain intangible something which has been dubbed an "academic air." It is the latter which is most harmful because it often fixes a gulf between teacher and learner, and the warmth and interaction of interest so essential to successful pedagogy are destroyed.

The second error into which an instructor often falls is teaching the same material in the same way year after year. The world changes and scholarship must change with it; the teacher changes and his teaching methods should also change. Variety and progress in teaching are even more important to the instructor than to his students, because the student is probably meeting the material for the first time and can therefore maintain a certain amount of interest in it, while the instructor has grown so stale on the subject that he has lost much of his desire to teach it and fails to challenge the student as he once did. This error may be remedied in many ways: textbooks may be changed, approaches might be varied, and definite programs of study leading to better acquaintance with one's field could be adopted. The methods suggested in this volume provide diversity of approach in Bible teaching; programs of study must be developed along individual lines. For instance, a friend of the writer utilizes what seems to be a workable plan for teaching books of the Bible: every time he teaches a book he has previously taught, he reads through two commentaries which he has not studied before.

Now that we have considered what a teacher should or should not be or do, it is time to discuss the question of the teacher's self inventory. He must constantly be a judge of himself. This can be done by a careful consideration of his product, the student. Does the student display characteristics worth admiring or those which are to be avoided? Is he a success or failure and why? How much of what he now is may be attributed to his teachers? Is the part that may be so attributed admirable? If a manufacturing concern is judged by the success of its product, might it not be fair to evaluate the teacher in the same manner.

Another way in which a teacher may judge himself is by observation of his methods. Can he see weaknesses in them? How well do students take to them? Does the pupil act alive and interested during the class period? A third method of self-judgment is through the administration of formal teacher-rating tests (this applies particularly to Bible institute or college work). Many such tests have been devised and are available at reasonable rates. On these blanks the student is given opportunity to comment (without disclosing his identity) on such items as the appearance of the teacher, fairness in grading, sufficiency of visual materials, preparation of the instructor, and adequacy of the textbook. If a teacher does not wish to use one of these formal ratings, he could mimeograph one of his own.

Yet another gauge of a teacher's work is the attendance in his classes. This would not be a criterion for required courses in college, but nearly every college or Bible institute teacher has some elective courses; and all of the Sunday-school attendance is on a voluntary basis. Let the Sunday-school teacher carefully survey the number of absentees and reason for absence, and let the week-day teacher observe the interest manifested in his elective courses.

Self-evaluation has one aim: the making of a better teacher. Every teacher should make steady improvement, and everyone should have a definite plan for improvement. Basic to such a plan is constant study of course content in order that the individual may know better the general materials and also that he may keep abreast of new developments in his field. Second, he will engage in experimentation of method of presentation and will in that way come to realize which types of approach are most effective. A careful study of teacher-rating results is of great value in determining points wherein one's weaknesses lie; it is at these points where diligent work should be done. Another source of improvement is through the help of others. One can ask the advice of other teachers, of his dean of education, or of his Sunday-school superintendent; he can make an effort to observe the teaching methods of others; or he may read helpful books on the subject.

General Instructional Principles

Before the methods which an instructor may utilize in presenting a lesson are discussed, consideration will be given to some of the principles which should guide each teacher in his work. That there are such principles which deserve avid attention on the part of the Christian instructor seems almost self-evident, yet there are many who have not caught the vision of the need for following these laws. To such, John Milton Gregory, former president of the State University of Illinois, ex-commissioner of the civil service of the United States, and a Baptist minister, has the following to say:

> But the most serious objection to systematic teaching, based on the laws of teaching, comes from Sunday-school men, pastors and others, who assume that the principal aim of the Sunday-school is to impress and convert rather than to instruct; and that skilful teaching, if desirable at all, is much less important than warm appeals to the feelings and earnest exhortations to the conscience. No one denies the value of such appeals and exhortations, nor the duty of teachers, in both day-schools and Sunday-schools, to make them on all fit oppor-

tunities. But what is to be the basis of the Sunday teacher's appeals, if not the truths of Scripture? What religious exhortation will come home with such abiding power as that which enters the mind with some clear Bible truth, some unmistakable "Thus saith the Lord," in its front? What preacher wins more souls than Moody with his open Bible ever in hand? What better rule for teacher or pupil than the Master's "Search the Scriptures"? What finer example than that of Paul who "reasoned" with both prejudiced Jews and caviling Greeks "out of the Scriptures"? If the choice must be between the warmhearted teacher who simply gushes appeals, and the cold hearted who stifles all feeling by his icy indifference, give me the former by all odds; but why either? Is there no healthful mean between steam and ice for the water of life? Will the teacher whose own mind glows with the splendid light of divine truths, and who skilfully leads his pupils to a clear vision of the same truths, fail in inspirational power? Is not the divine truth itself—the very Word of God—to be credited with any power to arouse the conscience and convert the soul?

These questions may be left to call forth their own inevitable answers. They will have met their full purpose if they repel this disposition to discredit the need of true teaching-work, in Sunday-schools as well as in common schools; and if they convince Sunday-school leaders that the great natural laws of teaching are God's own laws of mind, which must be followed as faithfully in learning his Word as in studying his works.[2]

Basic to all systematic teaching is *aim*. One must know where he is going if he intends to arrive. It is unthinkable that a soldier in the armed forces of the United States would be allowed to engage in warfare without having learned how to aim his gun and to hit his objective; just so, the Christian teacher who participates in Christian warfare needs to develop a good aim and facility for achieving that aim. In general the purpose of Christian teaching is threefold: to bring the pupil to Christ, to build him up in Christ, and to send him forth to work for Christ. But every lecture, discussion, or semester course has its own peculiar objectives; and the instructor is responsible for thinking these through very carefully before entering the classroom.

Fully as important as the instructor's development of aims is his understanding of the nature of education. To begin with,

[2] John M. Gregory, *The Seven Laws of Teaching* (New York: The Pilgrim Press, 1886), pp. 11, 12.

it must be stated that a person cannot be said to possess an education if he has only met the requirement of memorizing a certain amount of factual material, because this data may have no particular meaning for him; and if some of the facts do have a significance, they still are of little import to the individual until he has learned to integrate the details to which he has been exposed. Understanding and integration, then, are requisites to education. Moreover, the teacher needs to see that the student cannot receive an education from him. As Elbert Hubbard has said, "Education is a conquest, not a bequest — it cannot be given; it must be achieved."[3] This achievement is accomplished not by the transference of information but by the joint enterprise of a group who like mental activity, by the careful guidance on the part of the teacher of the students entrusted to his care until those students have thought into their own understanding new ideas or truth. Furthermore, the individual is not really educated until the principles he has imbibed have found practical relationship to everyday living; we are not dealing merely with a matter of books and schools. "The truly learned person has attained more than knowledge. He has good habits, specific skills, clear understandings, enduring interests, desirable attitudes, worthy purposes and noble ideals. All of these he translates into right conduct as he lives from day to day."[4]

A third important principle of effective teaching is the realization that the instructor's point of departure is always the needs, interests, and purposes of the individual pupil. If he is to understand these three factors, he must come to know his students: their maturity, attitude toward learning, previous study in the field, their problems, and aspirations. Since learning has its origin in a sense of need, he may often find it necessary to lead the student to a realization of his needs. In connection with the matter of coming to know one's students, it is interesting to comment on the experience of Ezekiel. Before he was commissioned to be an effective

[3] C. B. Eavey, *The Art of Effective Teaching* (Grand Rapids: Zondervan Publishing House, 1953), p. 149.

[4] *Ibid.*, p. 215.

"watchman unto the house of Israel" (Ezek. 3:17), he "sat where they sat" (3:15).

Closely connected with the last principle is the matter of relating new material to the pupil's apperceptive mass: that is, new thoughts should be presented in terms of what he already knows and has experienced. In other words, the order of instruction is from the concrete to the abstract, from the familiar to the unfamiliar. It is of utmost importance that strange ideas and facts be made as intelligible as possible.

While other appeals have not been wanting, it seems that the emphasis in this study has been on the intellectual. The teacher should not allow himself to fall into such an error, however, because the whole man must be educated: the mind, the emotions, and the will. "If the intellect is misinformed, the feelings incite the will to do the wrong thing."[5] Further, "the intellect loads the gun, the will pulls the trigger, but the feelings direct the aim."[6] Great profit will accrue to the instructor who takes time to learn something of the workings of the mental, emotional, and volitional aspects of man and ways of meeting problems in connection with their expression. Ample are the educational psychology books in the average city library, and the interested teacher may find help there.

Something has been said earlier about the importance of planning a course, but this all-important subject deserves further comment. Many have the impression that they have prepared for a class when they have enough material to fill in the time, but of far more importance than consuming time is effective organization of what is to be presented. Of course, planning must begin long before the start of a semester or quarter. Lay out the whole course and assign proportionate time to each phase. Too much time spent on early phases prevents completeness and causes lack of perspective; magnification of certain details obscures some of the chief values. Demonstrate foresight by showing ahead of time how

[5] E. W. Thornton, *How to Teach.* Revision by C. J. Sharp (Cincinnati: Standard Publishing Co.), p. 17.
[6] *Ibid.,* p. 23.

a given assignment is important and where the students are going. Relate specific lessons to the over-all view. If possible, begin each class period with a summary of the ground to be covered. Six steps may be followed in organizing class programs:

1. Have an aim
2. Decide on a method to be adopted
3. Outline the lesson
4. Compose helpful questions
5. Select illustrations
6. Develop applications

Illustrations chosen as lesson helps may be either verbal or visual. The former are most effective if they are drawn from personal experience. (Naturally that would not be the case if the lecture were on a subject like history or literature; the observation was designed primarily for the Bible teacher). Visual illustrations consist of maps, charts, objects, pictures, models, film strips, and films. Of course, no special instructions can be given in this connection here because each hour of discussion has different needs; but one should make sure that visual aids are appropriate, that they are sufficient but not overly used, that they are visible to all in the room, and that they are related to the lesson material under consideration — rather than serving as mere entertainment.

Important to the successful handling of any course is the training of students to a correct use of books in the field. Make sure that they know the basic bibliography and the relative merits of each, along with a few salient facts about the more outstanding authors. Show the pupils how to use textbooks — the index, the table of contents, glossaries, graphs, footnotes, references, sectional and topical headings, etc. See that they are able to use properly dictionaries, encyclopedias, reference works, and all available sources of materials. A simple plan for cursory consideration of a book might include the following:

1. Note the author, title, place and date of publication, edition, and number of pages.
2. Outline the author's background, theological position, etc.
3. Briefly state the aim of the book.

4. Jot down significant ideas and/or quotations.
5. Evaluate the book. Did it fulfill its aim? What are your general reactions?

One of the easiest ways of composing such a report is to read carefully the preface, table of contents, and the first chapter; in the second and following chapters, read the first paragraph and the first sentence of each succeeding paragraph.

Just as the conclusion is vital to a successful sermon, so the fixing of the impression is necessary to a well-taught lesson or course. Often this important factor is neglected. Impressions have been fixed along the way if the important points were effectively emphasized and understood, but if there is any doubt, take a little time for review; let the class ask questions; and describe again the outstanding problems or the facets of a single problem.

When a unit or a course has been taught, it is time for a test. Remember that tests are not given for the mere purpose of assigning a grade or making a student work. They have a value of demonstrating the difficulties the student is facing; they tell the teacher where instruction has not been clear; and they show how well the student has measured up to what was expected of him. A great achievement has been scored if the instructor can so construct a test as to lead the student into a greater understanding of the course material; this can be done if the questions demand a reintegration of facts that were covered during the course.

Before leaving the general subject of teaching principles, it may be well to note the seven laws of teaching as set forth by Gregory:

(1) A *teacher* must be one who knows the lesson or truth to be taught.
(2) A *learner* is one who attends with interest to the lesson given.
(3) The *language* used as a medium between teacher and learner must be common to both.
(4) The *lesson* to be learned must be explicable in the terms of truth already known by the learner — the unknown must be explained by the known.
(5) *Teaching* is arousing and using the *pupil's mind* to form in it a desired conception or thought.
(6) *Learning* is thinking into one's own understanding a new idea or truth.

(7) The *test and proof* of teaching done — the finishing and fastening process — must be a reviewing, rethinking, reknowing, and reproducing of the knowledge taught.[7]

METHODS OF PRESENTING THE LESSON

In brief we have considered the qualities of a good teacher and some principles which contribute to his effective instruction; we turn now to a discussion of the ways in which he can present the material that he wishes to impart. Most prominent among the traditional types of teaching is the lecture method, but it is not necessarily the best under all circumstances, and its value is sometimes disputed. On the positive side, it economizes time, makes possible the summary of material, provides information not already known by the group and not easily accessible, and furnishes a means of giving the pupil proper perspective. Negatively, it enlists only a minimum of participation, denies the student sufficient contact with material to be studied, does not take into account individual differences, requires a great deal of skill in public speech on the part of the teacher, and tends to monotony more quickly than some other methods.

To be successful, the lecturer must catch the attention of the class and hold it; he must impress the memory of class members; and he must lead them to positive convictions and stir them to profitable action on the basis of those convictions. The correct use of the voice is very important in lecturing: employ emphasis but do not shout at students; watch speed; insert effective pauses; dictate clearly anything important enough for the student to transcribe but do not dictate or read too much — most of the time should be spent in merely talking, commenting, discussing, and explaining. Despite some of the difficulties faced in using the lecture method, many teachers feel that with slight variations they will get along better with this instructional approach than with any other.

A second commonly employed teaching device is the discussion. This may consist of the presentation of a problem by a leader with a group effort to discover its solution, or

[7] Gregory, *op. cit.*, pp. 5, 6.

a panel may consider a subject in the presence of a larger audience. To insure a really good discussion, there must be a leader who is a clear thinker, impartial, patient, self-controlled, well-versed on the subject, and possessed of a sense of humor. While this method is essential to good pedagogy, it often does not accomplish its intended goal because of failure on the part of the teacher to heed the following principles characteristic of good discussions.

1. The question under consideration should be clear to the participants.
2. The issue must be sufficiently vital to warrant spending time on it.
3. The discussion should not be allowed to degenerate into idle talk.
4. The leader should prevent a few from monopolizing the discussion.
5. Keep irrelevant issues at a minimum.
6. Allow only one person to speak at a time.
7. Instruct those participating to address themselves not to the leader but to the group.
8. Avoid debate unless the discussion has been planned for that type of procedure.

The *sine qua non* of a discussion period is a high degree of proficiency in the art of interrogation on the part of the group leader. His questions should be brief, simply stated, clear, and relevant. Clarence Benson suggests several practices to avoid when asking questions:

1. Avoid reading questions.
2. Avoid phrasing a question in such a way that it suggests the answer.
3. Do not ask a question which may be answered with "yes" or "no" unless you require proof for the answer.
4. Do not name the pupil before asking the question because it only embarrasses him and relieves the rest of the class from giving any thought to it.
5. It is a mistake to ask questions in a given order so a student will know when his turn will come.[8]

The question and answer method, sometimes called the tutorial approach, was very well developed by Socrates, who utilized interrogation to expose ignorance and pierce pretensions and then by further questioning to lead the student into the knowledge of the truth.

In addition to these ways of presenting lesson material are

---

[8] Clarence H. Benson, *The Christian Teacher* (Chicago: Moody Press, 1950), pp. 131-33.

the recitation, supervised study, and project methods. In the first of these, a student is questioned on specific material which he has been asked to learn. Observations already made on effective questioning may be brought into play here. One of the main purposes of this approach to learning is to clear up misunderstandings and lack of perception in the minds of the students while at the same time providing for them a good review. Supervised study is practiced in order to answer the questions of the pupil as they arise and to help him to develop good study habits. The project method is based on the maxim that we learn by doing, and a high level of interest in a subject usually can be maintained in this way because learning thus becomes fun. A word of caution must be issued here, however, lest the teacher allow too much emphasis upon activity rather than upon the truth to be learned. Teachers often fail to utilize the project method to its fullest because it requires greater skill on their part and more preparation than is true with many of the other approaches to the learning process.

It will probably take very little reflection to see that the best kind of teaching capitalizes on the value of variety and therefore utilizes a combination of every conceivable instructional device.

Two Basic Types of Bible Teaching

As the Bible teacher or pastor engages in classroom ministry, he will find that there are two basic types of Bible teaching: extensive and intensive, or survey and analysis. Both are essential to effective, well-rounded Christian growth. Too much emphasis on the former will result in superficial knowledge of the Word; too great attention given to the latter will cause the student to miss an over-all view of Scripture while he is engaged in learning in detail certain short passages.

Bible survey is not merely wandering through a book and commenting on items which seem significant to the teacher; it is a carefully planned presentation of fact relative to a specific book of the Bible, in an effort to lead the student into an understanding of the form, content, and general introductory matters concerning it. There is no regular procedure to follow in constructing the outline for teaching of this type, but the plan might well include the following items: name, authorship, date, occasion, destination, key verse, literary style, outline and survey of contents, important chapters, special problems, canonicity, interpretation, the Christological element, and relationship to other Bible books. Of course, the list would vary according to individual books. Sometimes the teacher will prefer simply to lecture on each of these subjects, but he may discover that short lesson periods prevent adequate discussion and that he will do much better work if students are provided with brief mimeographed notes that can serve as a basis of discussion. College and Bible institute students also appreciate some sort of outline or syllabus to facilitate their note taking and study, but this should not be so extensive as to constitute printed lectures or so extensively used as to destroy interest or spontaneity.

For the most part Bible analysis should be prefaced with a brief consideration of subjects listed as essential to a complete synthetical discussion. Then careful study and outlining should be done, as suggested in Chapter IV. The investigation of the book will be more meaningful to the student if points in the outline are emphasized as new units of the book are brought into purview. Probably a mimeographed outline would serve as a very real instructional benefit. As each portion of the book is considered, try to find a verse which will serve as a key for that section. Let the message of each part of the book be studied in relation to original languages, history, archeology, or anything else that may bear on the complete understanding of Scripture; and make sure that sufficient illustrations are used to illuminate and emphasize truth and to hold interest. And since facts are of no value by themselves, seek always to apply the teaching to spiritual life and development.

TEACHING METHODS DEVELOPED AND UTILIZED IN HISTORY

No consideration of methods of teaching would be complete without some reference to the manner in which such methods were used by great leaders in history, and especially by people of the Bible. While it is true that teaching devices in the Old Testament antedate the work of the Greeks, the plan of arrangement to be followed here is to group all of the Biblical materials together following the discussion of Greek teachers of the classical period. While the writer recognizes that there have been great educational leaders in medieval and modern times, it is felt that the present purpose is served by a brief treatment of the period up to and including the New Testament.

Among the earliest of the great Hellenic instructors were the Sophists, who flourished about the middle of the fifth century b.c. These teachers of a superior grade aimed primarily to prepare their students for civic life, rather than a specific profession. They endeavored to provide a general or liberal education to supplement the customary education of the day. Although they were rather successful in training men in oratory and disputation and thus enabling them to be civic leaders, they were skeptical or agnostic in most of their attitudes toward knowledge and tended to destroy the intellectual certainty and to undermine moral standards of the age in which they lived. Their teaching was conducted in large measure by means of lectures.

Socrates (c. 469-399 b.c.), while sometimes classed with the Sophists, really differed from them greatly in that he considered the arrival at truth to be the right end of intellectual effort rather than success in public life; but he, too, was skeptical in his approach. He and his method are known to us through the writings of Plato. Some have felt that Plato created the personage of Socrates in order that he might use him as a mouthpiece. Be that as it may, Socrates is given credit for developing the tutorial method or question and answer method. His practice was to question someone and then to show by further questions the inadequacy of the answer, meanwhile guiding the individual toward a sounder position. In this approach individual contact and adaptability are essential.

Plato (428-347 b.c.) taught more systematically than Socrates. He used an examination system and was more selective in his choice of students. He laid down principles which all would accept and built on them in such a way as to lead the student into more profound ideas; so they were not thinking their own thoughts as exclusively as in the Socratic approach.

Aristotle (384-322 B.C.) established an academy something like a modern research institute. Here he combined lecture with class discussion and experimentation. In his teaching he set out a series of topics which together formed a complete survey of a subject and then took each topic separately, broke it into a number of problems and examined each, all the while working toward a solution. He utilized abundant illustrations.

Let us turn now to teaching and teaching methods as observable in the Bible. Everywhere we look in the Old Testament,[9] we see God utilizing all available means for reminding the people of their relationship and obligation to Him. With the Jews generally education was a primary means of promoting their faith among the rising generation. Since the Jews were not largely literate, much of the instruction imparted was oral or by means of object lessons or special observances. Memorial instruction was employed in Joshua 4: 1-9. As the Israelites crossed over Jordan into the Promised Land, they picked up twelve stones, one for each of the tribes, and piled them up and left them there. When one asked the purpose of the heap, the nation's history was given him. Antiphonal rehearsal took place in Joshua 8:12-35 and Deuteronomy 27:9-26. In this case, half of the people were to stand on Mt. Gerezim, mount of blessing, and half on Mt. Ebal, mount of cursing. Then the Levites chanted the blessings and cursings and were answered after each phrase by an "amen" on the part of the people.

In Nehemiah 8, Ezra and Nehemiah conducted something of a street school as the people gathered in the street and listened to the reading and expounding of the Law from morning until noon for seven days. Weekly Sabbath instruction was also of prime importance. Not only did the Sabbath have instructional value, but so did the observance of a

---

[9] For information on Old Testament teaching and Paul as a teacher, the writer is indebted to Professor Douglas Cravens of Temple Baptist Theological Seminary.

number of other special days and ceremonies. In this connection note the redemption of first-born male children, circumcision, the weaning feast, keeping the Passover, offering of the first born of flock and herd, the feasts of Pentecost, Tabernacles, and Day of Atonement, the Sabbath and Jubilee years, and all of the offerings so carefully outlined in the early chapters of Leviticus.

Consider also the home training as reflected in Proverbs 22:6, "Train up a child in the way he should go, and even when he is old he will not depart from it" and in Deuteronomy 6:7, "And thou shalt teach them diligently unto thy children, and shalt talk of them when thou sittest in thy house, and when thou walkest by the way, and when thou liest down, and when thou risest up."

An ingenious device for reminding the people of the claims of the Word upon them was the use of phylacteries or prayer bands consisting of short extracts from the Law, which were worn around the forehead and on the left wrist by males over thirteen while they were in prayer (Ex. 13:9; Deut. 6:8).

The Tabernacle, Temple, and synagogue had a very important instructional value for the Jews, too. The latter was of special worth. Developed during the exile, the synagogue served as the preserver and promulgator of Jewish life and doctrine during the difficult days in Babylon and the following years of rehabilitation in the land, to say nothing of the many centuries since that time. In addition to the school sessions held during the week, Sabbath services provided a very real instructional means for the people. During a typical service there would be the reading of the Law and Prophets, prayers and benedictions, and a discourse on the Scripture read for that day.

As we proceed to a study of the New Testament, we concern ourselves primarily with the greatest teachers of all time — Jesus and Paul; but other teachers are to be found there, and these will be briefly mentioned. Among the Jews there was no higher title of honor than that of rabbi, and this epithet is applied to Jesus about sixty times in the New Testament. Earlier in this chapter the importance of specific aims in teaching was emphasized, and we see that the Master Teacher developed His instruction in line with several very excellent purposes: (1) to form right ideals; (2) to convert the soul; (3) to improve human relationships; (4) to meet life problems; (5) to grow mature character; and (6) to train for service.[10] Jesus' ministry was guided not only by high aims but by superior principles as well. These Dr. Price lists as follows: He (1) took the long look — saw the future possibilities of His followers instead of their present capabilities; (2) stressed the personal touch; (3) began where the people were and injected His principles into the situation which He faced, rather than teaching principles and then looking for the application; (4) stayed with vital matters; (5) worked on the conscience; (6) drew out the best; and (7) secured His pupil's self-activity.[11]

Probably the two factors which most contributed to the effectiveness of Jesus' teaching ministry were His great knowledge of Scripture and His incomparable understanding of human nature and the art of handling men. These are demonstrated constantly in the several teaching methods which He employed. Let us now look briefly at each of these methods.

1. *Speeches or discourse.* He read Scripture and expounded it in the synagogues; He delivered speeches in the open air, notably the Sermon on the Mount and the Olivet Discourse; and He taught a select group on frequent occasions.

2. *The story method.* Supreme examples of the omniscience of Jesus were the parables He uttered. These earthly stories with a heavenly meaning were usually clear enough in their general teaching, but they served to hide deeper truth from His opponents. While this type of instructional device may not seem to be the best to the Western mind, it must be remembered that parables and riddles are commonly used in the Near East even today; and in addition to that fact, they served a divine purpose.

10 J. M. Price, *Jesus the Teacher* (Nashville: The Sunday School Board, Southern Baptist Convention, 1946), pp. 31-44.

11 *Ibid.,* pp. 46-60.

3. *Dialogue.* Jesus was equally at home in dealing with a crowd or an individual. Note in this connection such examples as the Samaritan woman and Nicodemus.

4. *Disputation.* He was capable of meeting His enemies on their own terms and triumphed over them every time.

5. *Object lessons.* Perhaps a division should be made here between object lessons and miracles, but they may properly be classified together. The teaching effect is somewhat different in the lesson on humility taught by means of washing the disciples' feet and the lesson relative to Christ's deity presented at the healing of the paralytic borne of four, but the point was driven home with equal effectiveness in each case.

6. *Drama.* Jesus never put on a play for anyone, but He utilized to good effect the dramatic element. What could be more dramatic than the manner in which He restored Lazarus to life and the way in which He handled the raising of Jairus' daughter?

7. *Propagandizing.* Different from Socrates, Plato, and Aristotle, Jesus realized the importance and value of an organized missionary program by which His teachings could be disseminated far beyond the capabilities of His human frame. The three basic elements in propaganda which He utilized effectively were repetition, calling on a higher source of authority, and a clear indication of the activity He expected His followers to engage in.

Since the effectiveness of a teacher must be gauged by the results of his work, we would take it that Jesus was eminently successful; because His teachings transformed lives, led men to dedicate and sacrifice themselves to divine service, and influenced the literature, law, and art of every succeeding generation from that day until this.

Paul, like Jesus, was well prepared for his teaching ministry. He was trained in the Jewish faith by his parents almost from birth; surely this included a thorough knowledge of the Old Testament. He studied in Jerusalem under the tutelage of the great Gamaliel, and he very possibly may have attended the University of Tarsus during the some ten years of seclusion in that city prior to the first missionary journey. Moreover, he had a definite and abiding spiritual experience.

Paul took advantage of every opportunity of teaching the truth. Upon entering a town, his usual practice was to resort to the synagogue. He also carried on house to house visitation and teaching (Acts 20:20); instructed in private schools (Acts 19:9); taught in public places such as the Areopagus and the market place (Acts 17); took advantage of instructional opportunities while confined in his private house in Rome (Acts 28); and utilized correspondence for didactic purposes.

Paul, too, had well-developed aims. They may be listed briefly as follows:

1. laying the basis for intelligent conversion
2. providing a systematic understanding of Christianity
3. counteracting false philosophies
4. developing well-rounded Christian personalities
5. seeking to develop Christian citizens

Paul's primary teaching techniques were the lecture or didactic discourse, which he employed to advantage on Mars Hill or Areopagus (he possibly used the new Alexandrian rhetoric here), discussion or disputing (disputation in Acts 17:17 could possibly be construed as Socratic dialogue), letters, and example. The success of his teaching ministry is seen in that he laid the foundation of Christianity in a pagan world, formulated an orderly statement of Christian doctrine, and trained a group of leaders to carry on when he was gone. In this respect, we should note the Pauline method of multiplying his ministry, "And the things which thou hast heard from me among many witnesses, the same commit thou to faithful men, who shall be able to teach others also" (II Tim. 2:2).

In addition to the teaching ministry of Jesus and Paul, the New Testament demonstrates the fact that a number of others in the early Church engaged in this kind of activity. A partial listing of them includes: apostles (Acts 5:42); evangelists (II Tim. 4:4, 11); pastors (Eph. 4:11; I Tim. 3:2); Peter (Acts 2:40-42); John (Acts 4:1, 2); Barnabas (Acts 11:26); Apollos

(Acts 18:25); Priscilla and Aquilla (Acts 18:26); and Timothy (II Tim. 2:2).

CONCLUSION

We have considered at some length both methods of Bible study and teaching, but let us not be tricked by the Enemy of the truth into believing that our sufficiency lies in a mastery of the mechanics of methodology and our native talents. The statement of Jesus to the effect that "apart from me ye can do nothing" (John 15:5), should immediately renew our realization that our sufficiency is in Him alone. As Dr. Eavey says, the teacher is like the gardener: all of his careful efforts merely make it possible for plants to grow; he cannot impart life and cause growth — only God can do that.[12] We are merely vehicles; it is the Holy Spirit who is the real teacher; He must implant the truth within the individual heart and cause it to bring forth fruit. "Howbeit when he, the Spirit of truth, is come, he shall guide you into all the truth. . . . He shall glorify me: for he shall take of mine, and shall declare it unto you" (John 16:13, 14).

BIBLIOGRAPHY

Benson, Clarence H., *The Christian Teacher* (Chicago: Moody Press, 1950).

Betts, George H., *How To Teach Religion* (Nashville: Abingdon-Cokesbury Press, 1919).

Bower, W. C., *Christ and Christian Education* (Nashville: Abingdon-Cokesbury Press, 1943).

Cantor, Nathaniel, *Dynamics of Learning* (Buffalo: Foster & Stewart, 1946).

Deese, James, *The Psychology of Learning* (New York: McGraw-Hill, 1952).

Dewey, John, *How We Think* (Boston: D. C. Heath and Co., 1933).

Dobbins, Gaines S., *The Improvement of Teaching in the Sunday School* (Nashville: Sunday School Board, Southern Baptist Convention, 1943).

Eavey, C. B., *The Art of Effective Teaching* (Grand Rapids: Zondervan Publishing House, 1953).

————, *Principles of Teaching for Christian Teachers* (Grand Rapids: Zondervan Publishing House, 1940).

Gaebelein, Frank, *Christian Education in a Democracy* (New York: Oxford University Press, 1951).

————, *The Pattern of God's Truth* (New York: Oxford University Press, 1954).

[12] *Principles of Teaching for Christian Teachers*, pp. 9, 10.

Gregory, John M., *The Seven Laws of Teaching* (New York: Pilgrim Press, 1886).

Guthrie, E. R., *The Psychology of Learning* (New York: Harper & Brothers, 1952).

Haden, Eric G., *Educational and Evangelistic* (Kansas City, Kansas: Central Seminary Press, 1950).

Highet, Gilbert, *The Art of Teaching* (New York: Alfred A. Knopf, 1952).

Horne, H. H., *Jesus — the Master Teacher* (New York: The Association Press, 1920).

Kuist, Howard Tillman, *The Pedagogy of St. Paul* (New York: George H. Doran Co., 1925).

Mort, Paul R., and William S. Vincent, *Modern Educational Practice: A Handbook for Teachers* (New York: McGraw-Hill Book Co., Inc., 1950).

Mursell, James Lockhart, *Successful Teaching* (New York: McGraw-Hill Book Co., Inc., 1946).

National Society for the Study of Education, *Learning and Instruction. Forty-ninth Yearbook, Part I.* (Chicago: University of Chicago Press, 1950).

Price, J. M., *Jesus the Teacher* (Nashville: The Sunday School Board, Southern Baptist Convention, 1946).

Tead, Ordway, *College Teaching and Learning, A Plea for Improvement* (New Haven: Yale University Press, 1949).

Thornton, E. W., *How to Teach.* Revised by C. J. Sharp (Cincinnati: Standard Publishing Co.).

Weigle, Luther, *Jesus and the Educational Method* (Nashville: Abingdon-Cokesbury, 1939).

Woodruff, Asahel, *The Psychology of Teaching* (New York: Longmans, Green and Co., 1948).

Yoakam, Gerald Alan, and Robert G. Simpson, *Modern Methods and Techniques of Teaching* (New York: The Macmillan Co., 1949).

APPENDIXES

THE USE OF THIS BOOK IN THE CLASSROOM

In discussing the question of how to teach the methods outlined in this book, the writer does not propose to set forth what may necessarily be considered the best or only way but merely intends to report that which he has found to be successful. Since we are all constructed differently, a practice that is best for one teacher or class may not be best for another. But with the statement of a friend in mind — "I would go a long way to get a usable idea" — these words are set forth, with the hope that the reader can glean something of value for his own ministry.

As indicated in Chapter II, the inductive method requires an entire school term for adequate treatment. Suggestions for the development of a book from this standpoint were made in that chapter; so it will not be necessary to engage in that subject in detail here. It might be said, however, that very detailed planning on the part of the teacher is required for this method. First of all, he should study the book carefully and develop a complete outline in order that he will know how many sections of study for which to plan; the second step is to determine the number of class hours available during the term; then it can be decided how many hours should be devoted to each section of the book — sometimes it may be necessary to divide a section into units small enough for daily assignments. To prevent an over-abundance of that, however, the student may be assigned a whole section at a time and asked to do certain parts of a given list of instructions for each hour to be devoted to the section. If this plan is not followed, the student will soon lose the sense of unity and plan in the mind of the author when he wrote the book of the Bible. It would be a wise plan to issue a mimeographed set of instructions for the entire school term when the semester or quarter opens; then the student will never be in the dark as to what is required of him.

Now let us consider classroom management. It may be that the teacher will desire to begin the hour with a quiz over the unit assigned for that day. Whether or not he comes to this conclusion, he should begin the discussion with the effective naming of paragraphs and the section. Part of the hour may be devoted to questions listed on the mimeographed study guide or questions which reorganize in another way the information gleaned by the student in his carrying out of instructions given in the study guide. If there is time, pupils may wish to mention observations they discovered in their personal study. Something was said in Chapter II about charting findings, but it should be added here that charting usually goes more smoothly if a portion of the term has been allowed to elapse before such a project is begun; then the student has more background for use in comparison and tracing.[1]

The remaining methods of the book may be dealt with in a school term of two semester hours or three quarter hours. Such a term might well begin with a discussion of the necessity of the Holy Spirit's teaching ministry in pursuing Bible study. Something of this is intimated in Chapter I.

In general, the procedure during the term is to define the method, discuss a part or the whole of an example of the method, and make the assignment, in one hour; and to discuss the completed method in a later hour. Usually it is better to begin a class period with an explanation of the next assignment instead of a consideration of the assignment due, because frequently there is not time at the end of an hour to give adequate attention to the problems the pupil will have in working out the following assignment. The result will be that

[1] A booklet on Mark that will prove to be of help in the development of this method is Jane Hollingsworth's *Discovering the Gospel of Mark*, published by Inter-Varsity Christian Fellowship.

either he is not able to do the lesson well, or the teacher, realizing the quandary in which the student finds himself has to postpone the lesson for the following hour, and the whole schedule for the semester is destroyed.

In order to economize on time, the teacher will discover that completed assignments on some of the methods do not require class discussion; this is especially true with the scientific, cultural, and devotional approaches. Several hours might well be consumed on such methods as the biographical or analytical. For instance, about four periods are sufficient to deal with the biographical method, one hour each being devoted to the study of an individual in a single book, an individual as dealt with in all of Scripture, biographical narrative exposition, and character exposition.

The instructor probably will not deem it necessary to give any kind of quiz or examination during the term when the sixteen methods were taught because he can determine quite adequately from papers handed in whether or not the student has mastered the method sufficiently. In this connection it may be observed that a grade given for the memorization of principles which the student is unable to put into practice is not a fair indication of his knowledge of the field.

In conclusion, constantly drive home the challenge of using these methods after the course is over. Remember, principles inculated are merely blueprints to be used as a guide for constructing finished buildings.

Appendix II

EFFECTIVE OUTLINING

Outlining is the general sketching or delineation of a plan, course of procedure, or line of thought along which details are developed. Outlines are not ends in themselves, though the care and time consumed in composing them might lead the student to feel that they are. They are a means to an end — the providing of an organized plan of procedure. They are indispensable to orderly development of any subject, and they reveal much about the mental processes and abilities of the one constructing them. In line with the practical approach taken in this book, the whole subject of outlining is discussed here in some detail.

TYPES OF ARRANGEMENT

In preparing an outline, the student should remember that he needs to know not only how to construct an outline but what type to use. Various sequences may be followed in the process of organization. The first of these is the *time sequence* or chronological arrangement. For this, three possible directions might be followed: one may begin at a certain period or date and move chronologically to a conclusion, or he may start at the conclusion and move logically to the beginning, or he might adopt the *in medias res* procedure. The first two movements should be clear, but the third needs some clarification. This is a Latin phrase which means "in the middle of things." It is a device commonly employed in short stories, plays, and novels. A high point of interest during the life of an individual or movement is selected as a starting point for the story or outline; then the writer returns to the beginning of the history he is seeking to portray and brings it to its conclusion or to the point of development which the individual or movement has reached at the time of writing.

Another kind of arrangement is the *cause-effect sequence*, in which one discusses certain procedures or paths of action and the results that may be expected from following them. This development is especially effective for dealing with Bible biography studies. A third method of organization is the *topical sequence*. Doctrinal or theological studies are usually of this type, because they are best systematized by considering certain aspects of the over-all teaching. For instance, one would study the doctrine of God under such headings as "attributes," "trinitarian relationships," "names," and "relation to created beings." A fourth approach is the *geographical* or *space sequence*. Whole books, such as Exodus and Acts, are profitably studied from the standpoint of this type of organization; the life of Christ may also be approached in this manner, if one is interested in outlining the study according to ministry in Galilee, Samaria, Judea, and Perea. There is yet another outline form which is frequently utilized in general secular work and adaptable in a few cases for Bible study; it is the problem-solution type. The usual arrangement in this sequence is first to detail the problem and then to present and evaluate solutions.

HOW TO PREPARE AN OUTLINE

Outlines are developed primarily to aid in presentation of Bible truth; they must, therefore, be executed with a high degree of accuracy, practicality, and good form. It should be stated, however, that even if one is not organizing material for the purpose of dissemination, careful outlining will prove beneficial because it leads to more effective personal study and promotes better habits of clear and orderly thinking.

Naturally, procedures of outline preparation vary with the type and length of material to be outlined. Sometimes a teacher interests himself in organizing the study of an entire book for a semester or quarter of academic investigation; or he may have only a half hour to present a short topic to a Sunday-school group. Whether he is engaged primarily in the former or latter, certain basic principles will assist him.

1. The outline must center around a theme. If one chooses to outline an entire book, he must discover the central message of the book and endeavor to learn how each section of the book bears on that message. If a brief passage or a subject is to be detailed, the procedure is the same, with the exception that in the latter case care will be exercised to limit the topic to such an extent that no extraneous material unrelated to that topic remains among the notes taken in preparation for outlining.

2. Closely related to the first observation is the fact that an outline must be characterized by unity. Each of the main points of the outline should relate to the theme and be clear subdivisions of it. All sub-points must plainly connect with their respective main points.

3. Parallelism is also a mark of effective outlining. This applies to the phrasing of points as well as structural arrangement. In respect to the latter, it should be said that balance

must be maintained in that there never can be an *a* without a *b* or a *1* without a *2*. Balancing of phraseology consists of similarity of English form of all outline points in a given class. For instance, if *I* is stated in a complete sentence, the same will be true of *II, III,* and *IV.* The *A, B,* and *C* under *I* must be phrased the same, whether they are expressed as infinitive, participial, or gerundive phrases, or in some other way.

4. Another important factor to keep in mind when outlining is logical subordination. If there are too many main points in the outline, it is obvious that the organization is faulty and that some of the items should be sub-points. On the other hand, do not make something a sub-point when it is really a main subdivision of thought. For instance, if one were making an outline of the doctrine of God, *I* might be *Names of God;* and *II, The Trinity;* but *III* would not be *The Holy Spirit,* because that would be *C* under *II, A* and *B* being *Father* and *Son.*

5. A consistent set of symbols should be used in an outline. The procedure most widely employed is the alternation of numerals and letters as follows:

   I.
      A.
         1.
            a.
               (1).
                  (a).

It is not permissible to use letters under letters or numbers under numbers:

Wrong:	Wrong:
I.	I.
1.	A.
2.	a.
II.	b.
	B.

Occasionally a student, though adopting correct symbols, places all numbers and letters in his outline in the left margin instead of practicing proper indentation; this is to be avoided because it tends to obscure the logical relation of items.

Keeping in mind the types of arrangement and general suggestions for outlining, we are now ready to consider actual outline construction. After completing research and note-taking, the first step is to choose and limit the subject. Whether a whole Bible book or a brief topic is involved, one needs to take into account the time at his disposal, the attitudes and background of the audience, and the purpose or aim of the teaching or preaching. If a book is to be outlined, the procedure is very much circumscribed; but for other types of presentation, the next step is to list in general the main points to be covered. Third, one will rearrange these points according to a satisfactory sequence, after which he will insert sub-points. The latter usually consists of parts of a whole, lists of qualities, illustrative examples, items of proof or confirmation, and the like. The fourth step is to rephrase all points of the outline in good English, parallel in structure. Last, check over the entire outline to see if the subject is completely covered, or at least as nearly so as the purpose demands, and to determine whether the material summarized there can be covered in the allotted time and whether the finished product accomplishes the aim you wish to achieve in presenting it.

Appendix III

A BRIEF DIGEST OF THE SCIENCE OF HOMILETICS

The English term *homiletics* is derived from the Greek *homilia*, which is defined as "conversation," "mutual talk," "discourse," or "persuasion." This basic meaning has been expanded until the English word now signifies "the effective preparation and delivery of sermons."

There are three basic types of sermons: topical, textual, and expository. In line with its name, the first is developed around a topic that may occur to the mind of the preacher as a result of his Bible reading or study of other types of literature. While it is designed to present spiritual truth, it does not necessarily expound any particular passage of Scripture and may not even be related to a Bible text. The textual message is generally based on a Scripture portion and usually takes all of the main points from the text, but sub-points do not usually originate in the text. Expository sermons consist of several varieties, but all of them are directly related to Scripture and take the main points and sub-points from it; they endeavor to expound completely the text under consideration. Included in the list of expository sermon types are analytical, character, biographical, subject, and narrative sermons. Analytical exposition is the careful and complete treatment of a brief portion of Scripture; Chapter III of this book describes how one can effectively analyze Bible portions. Chapter VI tells about biographical and character sermons; Chapter VII details the approach for narrative exposition; and Chapter VIII suggests how subject exposition may be developed.

The question which now logically arises in the mind of the preacher is, How shall I go about choosing the type or content of my messages? By way of answer, a bevy of questions may be suggested as a criterion of judgment.

1. What kind of instruction do my people need most?
2. What have I tended to neglect in my preaching? Have I seemed to ride one subject too hard, with the result that my ministry is lopsided?
3. What am I best fitted to preach? That is to say, certain themes require great depth of spiritual experience on the part of the minister, and he might, well avoid them until he reaches a high point of spiritual maturity.
4. Are my people showing a real spiritual growth? If not, chances are that they need more of the expository type of message.

Of course this examination must be subordinated to the guiding ministry of the Holy Spirit, but all of us are aware that He uses circumstances in guiding us into His perfect will. Moreover, as the preacher stays in the Word, certain subjects will burn in his soul so forcefully that he will not be able to avoid them. Once the topic is chosen, the method of presentation must be decided upon. This is not a great difficulty because stories will be told according to the principles of narrative exposition; lives of Biblical characters will be dealt with in line with character or biographical exposition; doctrinal subjects will be detailed from the standpoint of subject exposition; and short

APPENDIXES   213

passages of Scripture may be preached as textual sermons or analytical exposition.

Once the subject is chosen and the method of presentation decided upon, the next step in preparing a sermon is to outline the body of the message. In this connection, principles relative to outlining as set forth in Appendix II should be kept in mind. Above all, be sure that the body of the message is united around one theme. Main points of the outline must be subdivisions of this thought, rather than separate sermons in themselves. In other words, when preaching, deliver one sermon on one subject and not on three or four diverse subjects. There is no law which dictates that a sermon have three points; let the text or subject determine that for you, and do not force a subject into three points when it should be two or four. Furthermore, alliteration in the outline is not necessary for the development of a successful product. Some ministers develop it naturally and enjoy using it, but those who find it difficult might better spend their time on the content of their sermons.

In developing the main portion of the message, be sure to include a sufficient number of illustrations of a type appropriate to the subject, occasion, and the audience. Someone has said that illustrations are the windows that let the light through; take care, then, that there be enough to shed adequate light on the subject, but not so many that the structure collapses from lack of proper roof and wall supports. Illustrations are usually most effective when they arise from one's own experience or study instead of being borrowed from a book of illustrations.

When the body of the message is complete, it is time to consider appropriate introductions and conclusions. Basically, the purpose of the introduction is to introduce the subject, but the introduction should be made in such a way as to engage interest in the subject and prepare the mind of the hearer to understand the truth which is to be presented, to appreciate its importance, and to accept its conclusions. When constructing an introduction, there are certain principles to keep in mind. One is not to draw attention to himself. Many a preacher prays in his introductory prayer that the speaker may be hidden behind the Cross and that Christ only shall be manifested; then he proceeds to tell about all of his illnesses, lack of time for preparation, and inabilities for preaching, with the result that the attention of the congregation is called to the speaker instead of his Lord. Often the Lord brings difficulties upon us in order to cause us to depend more fully on Him; certainly He will care for all who lean upon Him, and we need not ask for human sympathy from the pulpit.

The introduction should consist of a single thought closely related to the theme of the discourse; a variety of ideas incorporated into an introduction will not prepare the mind of the listener for the subject of the body of the message. It should not be too long and it should not promise too much. Many introductions create the impression that a second Demosthenes has come to town; and after three minutes all know he has not, because the initially high tone is gone; the preacher simply could not keep up the pace. In addition, make the approach friendly but not gushy.

Numerous are the sources of introductions; some of the more important are listed here:

1. Note the text or context. A verse or passage to be expounded will be quoted, or the context explained.
2. Use the problem approach. Ask a leading question or present a vital problem.
3. Make a direct statement of purpose.
4. Deliver a striking quotation.
5. Give an illustration.
6. Refer to a current news item.
7. Discuss the occasion of the meeting — baccalaureate, Thanksgiving, devotional, New Year watch-night service.
8. Report a life situation — "The other day when I was riding on a street car, I heard a woman say to her companion. . . ."
9. Utilize Biblical customs.
10. Develop the geographical or historical setting.

Of prime importance in sermon preparation is the conclusion. Comments Dr. William Evans, "The Greek orators expressed their conception of the importance of the conclusion of an address, or oration, by calling it, 'the final struggle which decides the conflict.' It is not too much to say that the last five minutes of the sermon is the most important part of it. It is during this time that the issues involved are decided, if decided at all. Yet, how very seldom the conclusion receives the preparation and thought it ought to by virtue of its important place. Very often its matter and form are left to the inspiration(?) of the moment. How scattering, and wild, and pointless are the 'concluding remarks' of the average sermon — what aimless exhortations! This is sad, indeed, when we remember that we have been speaking for thirty or forty minutes for the very purpose of accomplishing the work of the last five minutes. The Introduction and the Body or Argument of the sermon, with its definition, explanation, proof, and argument, have all been dealt with for the very purpose of bringing things to an issue in the Conclusion. What a mistake then to neglect the thorough preparation of this important part of the sermon."[1]

Granting that it is important to prepare the conclusion carefully, let us note a few principles to keep in mind while making that preparation for and delivering the finished product. First, be simple. If you are trying to convince a congregation concerning a basic truth, do not hinder your work by uncommon vocabulary, flowery style, and ambiguous phraseology. Second, make the conclusion single. Just as the introduction should suggest a single subject and the body of the message will develop various aspects of that topic, so the conclusion has a responsibility of clinching that one idea in the minds of the hearers. Third, make the conclusion personal; do not allow it to be too general or vague. Fourth, just as with the introduction, continued effectiveness of the ending of a sermon may be enhanced by utilizing a variety of conclusions. Fifth, never apologize for personal failures during the course of the message nor call attention to yourself in other ways. Sixth, avoid humor; this is a sacred moment — jokes will destroy a spiritual atmosphere. Last, abstain from the rather common practice of saying frequently near the end of the message, "Now to con-

[1] William Evans, *How to Prepare Sermons and Gospel Addresses* (Chicago: Bible Institute Colportage Assoc., 1913), p. 107.

clude." If you do make such a statement, bring the sermon to an end soon thereafter. It might be wise, however, to come to a conclusion without a reference to the fact; the attention of the audience is often held better in that way.

In the last paragraph the use of a variety of conclusions was urged; now it remains to point out the kinds of endings that may be employed.

1. The direct appeal. On the basis of what has been said in the earlier part of the message, ask the individual to make certain decisions or perform given duties.
2. Summary of the main points of the message.
3. A poem or verse of a song which embodies the most significant elements of the sermon.
4. An illustration appropriate to the theme.
5. A carefully composed concluding sentence or Scripture verse.
6. Contrasting truth. For instance, if the entire message has been given over to a description of heaven, the conclusion might be devoted to a brief statement about eternal punishment.
7. The missing conclusion. Sometimes it is extremely effective to stop suddenly after the last major point of the sermon and, as it were, leave the point and the audience hanging in the air. The instruction might have a greater impact upon the mind of the hearer if he is left to draw his own conclusions.

After the message has been developed and the introduction and conclusion affixed, the question of delivery arises. While three methods of presentation are usually listed, the enumeration possibly may be expanded to five. Occasionally a minister is called upon to deliver a message with almost no warning at all. If he speaks, it may then be said that he is preaching an *impromptu* sermon. Of course this kind of practice is possible only if the speaker engages in constant study of the Word. A few ministers choose to read their homilies; if they are exceptional they might hold the attention of the congregation, but this method usually kills the interest of the hearers. Fewer yet memorize their entire messages. The danger in such a case is that they might forget a part of the sermon and be unable to continue. As with the reading approach, the difficulty with this method is that it prevents sufficient flexibility to meet the exigencies of the hour. The fourth type of delivery is dubbed *extemporaneous*. In this case, thorough preparation is made, and the sermon may even be completely written out, but few if any notes are taken into the pulpit. The last type of delivery may be called the "combination" method. It is thoroughly prepared; parts of it — such as the introduction and conclusion — may be memorized; quotations may be read; and there is plenty of freedom to permit the inspiration of the moment.

If the reader is interested in going on from this brief introduction to a more thorough investigation of the field of homiletics, he will find many of the following standard works in the average Bible institute or Christian college library. Let it be said that no effort has been made to construct an exhaustive bibliography on the subject.

1. A. W. Blackwood, *The Fine Art of Preaching* (New York: Macmillan, 1937).
2. ————, *Planning a Year's Pulpit Work* (Nashville: Abingdon-Cokesbury, 1942).
3. ————, *Preaching from the Bible* (Nashville: Abingdon-Cokesbury, 1941).
4. John A. Broadus, *On the Preparation and Delivery of Sermons* (New York: Harper and Brothers, 1926).
5. William Evans, *How to Prepare Sermons and Gospel Addresses* (Chicago: Bible Institute Colportage Assoc., 1913).
6. F. B. Meyer, *Expository Preaching: Plans and Methods* (reprint; Grand Rapids: Zondervan Publishing House, 1955).
7. G. Campbell Morgan, *Preaching* (New York: Fleming Revell, 1937).
8. T. Harwood Pattison, *The Making of the Sermon* (Rev. Ed.; Philadelphia: American Baptist Publishing Society, 1941).
9. Jeff D. Ray, *Expository Preaching* (Grand Rapids: Zondervan Publishing House, 1940).
10. Charles Haddon Spurgeon, *Lectures to My Students* (reprint selected lectures from Series 1, 2 and 3; Grand Rapids: Zondervan Publishing House, 1955).
11. W. H. Griffith Thomas, *The Work of the Ministry* (Chicago: Moody Press, 1927).

APPENDIX IV

FILING

As the student pursues his acquisition of Biblical knowledge, he constantly discovers, in his Bible and in books, magazines and papers, items that should prove valuable to him in further study and in preparation to teach the Word. Often he will pose the question: How can I put these things away so I shall be able to find them again? It is the purpose of this brief treatment to answer such a question.

In constructing a filing system, certain basic principles should be observed:

1. The filing system should be characterized by simplicity. Complex filing systems require a considerable amount of business education on the part of the user and often demand more time and effort than they are worth to the student or teacher. Let it be remembered that a file is not an end in itself but a means to an end.

2. It should facilitate ease of locating material. Files are not worth much unless it is possible to find an item when it is desired. The system cannot, then, be too simple; it must not consist merely of a box full of folders alphabetically arranged and stuffed full of interesting clippings and jottings. There must be careful storing of articles and adequate attention given to cross references.

3. It should require a minimum amount of time for classifying materials. Many a student has allowed clippings and other items that should be in his files to gather in a box in the corner of his study — simply because it was much easier to allow them to collect until he had ample time to store them than it was to drop them in the file when he discovered them. The unfortunate factors involved in such a situation are that the individual is deprived of the use of these materials until they are filed and that if the stack grows too large, he will probably despair of ever putting it in any kind of order and throw it all away. A sufficiently simple system would facilitate immediate filing and avoid such a loss.

4. It should be maintainable at a minimum of expense. High-

priced equipment may often require such a large portion of the student's budget that he will find it impossible to purchase other much-needed supplies. Moreover, he may find it impossible to buy materials when needed and be forced to postpone the classifying of much valuable material.

It now remains to recommend a system that will measure up to these principles. Probably the most satisfactory development will contain four parts. (1) a 3" x 5" Scripture reference file; (2) a 3" x 5" subject file; (3) a series of 9" x 12" folders bearing names of books of the Bible; and (4) a series of 9" x 12" folders bearing subject titles.

Let us consider the 3" x 5" files first. It would be a wise plan to purchase a two drawer metal cabinet with over-all measurements of about 12⅜" x 7⅛" x 15". The left drawer could be used for a Scripture reference file and the right one for a subject file. For the left drawer purchase three sets of alphabetical tabs; these may be turned over and names of Bible books written on the other side. Short poems, quotations, sermon outlines, and the like may be stored here. Be sure to place the Scripture reference in the upper left corner of the file cards and arrange in numerical order. For the right drawer purchase one set of alphabetical tabs and arrange subject entries behind their respective letters; write the subject name in the upper left corner. If the time comes when many cards accumulate for the same subject, a tab bearing that heading may be inserted in the file. Be sure that adequate cross references are made between these two files; for instance, a poem placed under John 3:16 might be cross referenced under "belief" or "gospel." The student is encouraged to carry extra blank cards with him at all times. Then when he hears a lecture or a sermon or finds a good quotation while reading in the library, he can readily take notes, assign a title to the card, and deposit it in the correct place in the file upon returning home; it is then that the workability of this system will be demonstrated because the item can be as easily filed as stacked away for future filing.

The remaining two sections of the filing system now demand attention. One of these units will consist of sixty-six folders bearing the names of books of the Bible; these can be arranged in alphabetical or Biblical order. When too much information accumulates to be housed in one folder, a second may be added. The fourth part of the filing development is devoted to miscellaneous subjects — Biblical or otherwise — on which the student has too much material to be placed on a 3" x 5" card; these folders are arranged in alphabetical order. Here again, cross referencing is important. In fact, cross references must be established between all four parts of the filing program. File folders are available in various cuts — that is, a certain amount of the top of the folder is cut away, leaving the rest to serve as an identification tab. Usually, it is not a very good plan to use folders which might be classified as "one-cut," i. e., do not have any of the back cut away, because staggering of subject headings is then prohibited; and it is more difficult to read the file. Third-cut folders are recommended because they permit greater staggering of subject tabs, and the tabs are still wide enough for fairly long titles. Many prefer merely to write or print titles on the folders, but a much neater product is obtained if gummed labels are typed and affixed to the folders. Such labels are available in perforated sheets or rolls and in a wide variety of colors. While they demand a slight outlay, they save money in the long run because whenever one wishes to change the title on a folder, all he has to do is put on a new label; it is not necessary to throw away an old folder because a title cannot be erased.

While students are enrolled in school, they usually do not have adequate funds for filing cabinets; nor do they desire to have the responsibility of shipping large office furniture around the country when moving from one place to another. In such a case, file folders may quite satisfactorily be stored in wooden or even cardboard boxes; and card files may be housed in the boxes in which the cards were packaged when purchased, provided they were bought in lots of 1,000.

SUBJECT INDEX

Absalom, 58, 59
Acrostic, 92
Allegory, 99
Analogy, 100
Analysis defined, 33, 34
Antithesis, 102
Apostrophe, 101
Aristotle, 196
Babylon, 126-131
Bible
　Poetry, 90-94
　Prose, 94-96
　Teaching, 185-194
　Versions, 89
Biographical argument, 59
Biographical exposition, 53-59
　Biographical-narrative exposition, 54-56
　Character exposition, 56-59
Biographical narrative, 47-53
Charting, 18, 22
Criticism defined, 39
Culture defined, 133
David, 167-169
Egypt, 106-109
Epistemological problem, 151-153
Ethical problem, 153, 154
Filing, 218-220
Geography defined, 105
Government, Bible teachings on, 156-158
Hebrew music, 136-139
Historical problem, 154
Holy Spirit
　inspiration, 27
　outline of doctrine of, 80
　teaching ministry, 11, 13, 201
Homiletics
　See biographical exposition, narrative exposition.
　Appendix III, pp. 211-217

Hyperbole, 101
Inductive method defined, 16
Irony, 100
Jesus Christ, 77, 78, 82-85, 197-200
John the Baptist, 11, 21
Levirate marriage, 115, 116
Litotes, 102
Metaphor, 98
Metaphysical problem, 151
Metonymy, 102
Moses, 55, 56, 106
Narrative exposition, 64, 68, 69, 70, 71
Nebuchadnezzar, 126-131
Outlining, 17, 19, 27, 30, 37, 48, 207-210
Paul, 48-51, 200
Personification, 101
Philosophy defined, 149
Plato, 195
Political problem, 155, 156
Psychology defined, 160
Rhetorical question, 102
Ruth, 115-118
Saul, 167-169
Simile, 98
Sociology defined, 112
Socrates, 195
Synecdoche, 103
Synthesis defined, 25
Teacher, requirements for Christian, 179-184
Temptation, 85-87
Theological problem in philosophy, 150, 151
Theology, outline of, 77-80
Timothy, 52, 53

221

SCRIPTURE INDEX